Fit for My King

His Princess 30-Day Diet Plan and Devotional

SHERI ROSE SHEPHERD

Revell

a division of Baker Publishing Group
Grand Rapids, Michigan

Published by Revell
a division of Baker Publishing Group
P.O. Box 6287, Grand Rapids, MI 49516-6287
www.revellbooks.com

Printed in the United States of America

Library of Congress Cataloging-in-Publication Data
Shepherd, Sheri Rose, 1961–
    Fit for my King : his princess 30-day diet plan and devotional / Sheri Rose Shepherd
       p.   cm.
    ISBN 978-0-8007-1916-6 (cloth)
    1. Christian women—Prayers and devotions. 2. Christian women—Health and hygiene. 3. Reducing diets—Recipes. 4. Weight loss—Religious aspects—Christianity. I. Title.
    BV4844.S5335 2009
    242′.4—dc22   2009024035

09   10   11   12   13   14   15   7 6 5 4 3 2 1

Contents

Contents

Introduction

ost women look at me today and think I'm the lead commander of this diet war we can't seem to win. I speak at several women's conferences each year on a variety of topics; however, every time I'd share the part of my life of how God healed me from an eating disorder, helped me conquer chronic fatigue, and gave me the strength and wisdom to lose over fifty pounds and keep it off, the women would bombard me with a desperate cry to teach them how.

So, after ten years of addressing this topic, speaking to over half a million women across this nation, I felt the Lord leading me to share *His plan* for *His Princesses* to break free from this *"food issue"* and *"Barbie bondage"* so we can win this *Diet War* once and for all!

I know from personal experience what it's like to grow up in what society refers to as a *dysfunctional home*. (Today, there are so many dysfunctional families that much of the world has lost sight of what a healthy, functional family looks like.) My parents have been married and divorced three times each, and I've been a part of five blended families. My dad had an extremely violent temper, and my mom was paralyzed by emotional pain. Because they were always in one crisis situation after another, I never felt the freedom to go to either of them for comfort and direction. When I needed comfort, I found it in food. When I was in pain, I used drugs and alcohol to escape. By the time I was sixteen, I was addicted to both the food and the drugs. I made so many poor choices, burned so many bridges, and nearly destroyed my mind and body. I believed I was destined for destruction. I wanted desperately to crawl out of this deep, dark hole of despair, but the harder I tried, the deeper I fell into depression and the more I ate.

At the lowest point in my life, my stepmom Susie challenged me with a painful question. She asked me how long I was going to use my past as an excuse for the poor choices I was making. She shocked me with the truth that I could do nothing to change my past, but I could choose to make the right choices to change my future.

That painful truth empowered me to change almost everything about myself. Believe it or not, in just one year, I lost all my excess weight, I stopped using drugs, I changed my friends, I changed my attitude, I improved my grades, I changed my clothes and my hair color, and while I was in a "change mode," I even got a nose job.

I went from a drug-using, overweight, insecure junior in high school to a powerful, popular senior who had boyfriends, a local beauty title, and a much better place in life. It looked like I had it all, and to the outside world I did. There was only one piece missing from what appeared to be the perfect puzzle: no matter how much I projected a perfect life or look on the outside, on the inside I continued to die a silent and secretive death that no one could see but me.

I felt lonely even in a roomful of people. I battled with deep, hidden depression because money, things, worldly success, and beauty could only hide my pain—they could not heal my heart or rebuild what was broken in my life or nourish my soul.

An English teacher of mine was so frustrated with me that she told me I would never amount to anything in life, that I was born to be a loser. I was certain my teacher was right until I discovered God's grammar lesson for broken lives like mine:

Don't put a period where God has a comma,
Because He has a plan for every life He creates.

By the time I reached age twenty-four, I did not know how to deal with my feelings. How could I possibly tell anyone that the young woman who seemed to have it all still cried herself to sleep every night, just like she did when she was a little girl. If I went to a doctor for my emotional pain, he would look at my blessed life and give me a drug for depression. I couldn't tell my parents because I did not want to disappoint them, when they were so proud of all I had become. If I told my friends about my emotional pain and eating disorder, they would look at my successes and think that I was ungrateful. So I did what I had learned to do as a young girl; once again I ignored the warning signs. I covered them up by losing more weight, winning more pageants, making more money, setting more goals, and filling my schedule with excessive busyness so I wouldn't have time to feel any pain.

I was thrown out on the road of reality. This time my emotional pain was so severe that every part of my body was hurting. I had panic attacks, crying spells, loss of memory, and chronic depression. The original pain from my childhood that had given me the power to change my life as a teenager no longer worked.

I had no more strength or desire to fill the empty pages of my life. I felt as if I were at the end of my life's story. I could not decorate the pain I was feeling anymore. I thought out a way I could end my life quickly; I felt it would be better to die with the world thinking that I was successful than to disappoint them with the truth that I was a mess.

I checked myself into a hotel room and decided that I would take my life with sleeping pills. When I walked into the room, I threw myself on the floor and screamed at the top of my lungs, "God, do You exist? If You do, please show me!"

I immediately felt His presence in the room, comforting me. The next morning I was invited by a friend to his grandparents' house, and these were the missionaries who led me to the greatest crown of all, the crown of everlasting life. This couple had nothing in common with me, but they had the very thing I needed most—they had peace and purpose and joy. The way they lived for the Lord led me out of slavery from the lies of this world and into the truth of God's promises for my life. It has been a long journey to learn how to walk in the freedom and even harder to stay free, but today, praise be to God, I am completely free and at peace with who God has created me to be. In other words, no more "Barbie bondage," and the Diet War has been won!

If you're ready to let go of lies we women believe and find your true legendary beauty, then *Fit for My King* is designed for you to find the root cause of why you're battling with your body image and discover the keys to break free from food controlling your life. Together we will dine as if we are dining with our King. We will nourish our souls and renew our minds while learning to take care of our bodies (God's temple). You will find thirty *His Princess Daily Devotions*, *His Princess Prayers*, and *"Treasures of Truth for Today"*—along with some special *"Love Letters"* sprinkled throughout this book. I also added some amazingly delicious recipes in the back of this book for you to enjoy while you are losing weight.

Our God desires for His beloved daughters to experience good health and for their souls to soar. We can and will become the best version of ourselves as we commit the next thirty days to our King!

His Princess
Diet Plan

*Beloved, I pray that in all respects you may prosper and be in
good health, just as your soul prospers.*

3 John 2 NASB

His Princess Purpose

ost of us fight an ongoing battle in our minds about our body image. We wish our bodies would look a certain way, we'd like to maintain a certain weight, and none of us like ourselves when we are controlled by our cravings. In order to win this war with our weight, we need to set our minds on our royal call, not on our cravings. Our diets need to be about our desire to honor our King, not about denying ourselves certain foods.

Our beloved Queen Esther is an excellent example for us to follow. Her desire to become queen was not about herself; it was for the purpose of glorifying her King and ultimately saving her people. She did not need to be the prettiest in the land to feel good about who she was. Esther was on a mission to win the king's heart so she could save her people.

Can you imagine if our purpose for being our best was to show our King how much we love Him by taking care of His temple and to have enough energy to save the lost? What a legacy we would leave for the next generation.

Below are the best diet secrets ever shared because they are given to us by our Father in heaven according to His Word:

1. To Honor God

> *Don't you know that you yourselves are God's temple and that God's Spirit lives in you? If anyone destroys God's temple, God will destroy him; for God's temple is sacred, and you are that temple.*

> *1 Corinthians 3:16–17*

Most of us are likely to miss out on the power of the biblical word picture found in the above verse. Today temples have no real significance for most people in the community; but to God's chosen people, the temple was the lifeblood of the civilization. It was the source of power, direction, and protection. It was the most beautifully designed, painstakingly immaculate, awe-inspiring fixture in the entire culture. It was functional, holy, and artistic, all in one. Why would God use this spectacular man-made creation as a symbol for our earthly body? Because both are His chosen place of dwelling.

Let's do this to honor the one who gave His very life for us. Let's spend the next thirty days treasuring His temple—our bodies!

His Princess Prayer

Dear Lord,

I confess I cannot do this next thirty days without Your strength. Please give me the stamina to commit thirty days to dine with You. Help me to crave Your whole foods. Help me to hunger more for You than for food. I love knowing that Your Spirit lives in me. I choose by faith to commit my body, my mind, and my diet to You. I make a covenant with You on this day to fast off all foods for thirty days that hinder my strength and keep me from running my race of faith for You.

In Jesus' name I pray, Amen

2. To Experience Good Health

Beloved, I pray that in all respects you may prosper and be in good health, just as your soul prospers.

3 John 2 NASB

Our God, our *Daddy* in heaven, tells us in His Word that above all things He wants our souls to prosper and He desires His daughters to experience good health. He loves us so much that He addresses us as "beloved." Dream with me for a moment: what if all Christians took care of our bodies for the right reasons, the right way—through proper nutrition, exercise, and rest? The results would be amazing.

- Imagine our pastors, evangelists, and missionaries having the health and energy to finish their ministries strong. Studies show that only one out of ten pastors will still be in the ministry by the time they reach sixty years of age—physical and emotional burnout being the major causes.

- Think about how much money would be saved on medical bills and health insurance and how much we would enjoy our golden years in life if we invest in our health now.

- Can you envision what God's people could accomplish here on earth if the body of Christ had more energy and clear minds? We would have more involvement in all church ministries and our outreach programs and prayer teams. Even more, we could remember the sermons each Sunday if we started our morning with a nutritious meal and a good rest the night before.

When you think about it, Christians should be the healthiest, happiest people on earth! After all, we know where we're going. We have life's instruction manual (the Bible), and we serve a God who has shown us, through His Word, how to take care of His temple—our bodies. But only if we take the necessary steps to be healthy will we be able to enjoy the abundance God promises. Our bodies are the physical vessels that God uses while we're here on earth; we need to take care of them in honor of Him. Jesus Himself borrowed an earthly body while He was here on earth, and He wants to use you to accomplish even greater things than He did!

His Princess Prayer

Dear Lord,

I am ready to receive from You the gift of good health. I want my soul to prosper, and I want to walk in victory over sickness and exhaustion. I commit the next thirty days to rebuilding my body for Your glory, not mine.

In Jesus' name I pray, Amen

3. TO GAIN STRENGTH AND ENERGY

Happy is the land whose king is a nobleman and whose leaders feast only to gain strength for their work, not to get drunk.

Ecclesiastes 10:17 NLT[1]

If we were going to make this personal we would say to ourselves, "Happy will my home be when I act like a noblewoman and eat only to gain strength to care for my loved ones!"

In order to gain this strength and energy, we must look at our goals. If we are exercising and eating healthy to bring glory to ourselves, we will run out of willpower. But if we are eating healthy to gain the strength to complete the royal call on our lives and to bring glory to our King, we will see victory like never before.

His Princess Prayer

Dear Lord,

*I no longer want to feel drunk on the junk food
I eat. I want to gain strength by eating the food
You have prepared for my body to be healthy and
strong. May I be a noblewoman who does eat only
to gain strength to further Your kingdom here on
earth.*

In Jesus' name I pray, Amen

4. FOR AN ETERNAL PRIZE

*Don't you realize that in a race everyone runs, but only one
person gets the prize? So run to win! All athletes are disciplined
in their training. They do it to win a prize that will fade away,
but we do it for an eternal prize.*

1 Corinthians 9:24–25 NLT[2]

Here is where the rubber meets the road. Our God is asking
us to train our minds and our bodies like an athlete. However,
He is asking this for a divine purpose—He is requesting that
His Princesses train for the eternal race. All the Olympic medals
in the world won't mean anything on the other side of eternity.
Rewards here on earth can't change a life or get us into heaven.
Now, I am not against running worldly races and winning the

trophies of man if it is for God's glory and not our own. For us, His daughters, our purpose to go into strict training is to win lives to Christ!

His Princess Prayer

Dear God,

I commit to practice strict self-control over the next thirty days. May this thirty-day commitment I am making to You turn into a life that runs the race of my faith with endurance. In Jesus' name I pray, Amen

In closing out this section about our purpose I want to pray that God prepares your heart, your mind, and your spirit to experience His touch like never before and to enjoy the journey toward a new life . . . the abundant life you were destined to live!

His Princess Covenant Letter

ow that we have got our hearts and minds in the right place about our purpose for losing weight and becoming our best for our King, let's make a real commitment.

A written covenant with your Lord will help ensure your victory, because your new diet is a commitment of the heart to bring glory to your King. Now your body becomes about His glory and not yours! In Him you can conquer anything. In Him you will receive the fruit of the Holy Spirit and the power to become what He created you to be.

Write your covenant in your own words or use the words on the next page.

After it is written and signed by you and a witness, put it in a place where you can read it every day for the next thirty days.

His Princess Covenant Letter

Dear Lord,

For the next thirty days, I want to honor You with my body by fasting off all white sugar, white flour, artificial sweeteners, and other artificial food. I commit to give up any other food or drink that may harm my body. I give You control of what I eat and make a covenant with You to take care of Your temple (my body). I commit to eat well, get proper rest, and exercise to bring glory to You, not to myself. I ask that You give me the fruit of the Spirit, self-control. Help me be disciplined in my mind, my body, and my spirit.

I give You my word and promise to commit to the above for the next thirty days.

Date of_____ (and thirty days thereafter)

Signed_____

Witnessed by_____

His Princess 30-Day Plan for Victory

1. Read Your Daily "His Princess Devotion"

There are thirty devotions written for you to feed your soul and keep you inspired and committed to your diet. Each day you will find a new reason to take care of your body, mind, and spirit. There are also daily prayers, Treasures of Truth, and some action steps that will get you where you desire to be. Keep this book by your bed or wherever you like to read, and be sure to read first thing in the morning.

2. Find an Accountability Partner

This walk was never meant to be walked alone. Jesus sent his disciples out in twos. You and I need someone to hold us accountable during this next thirty days. Prayerfully consider the right person to ask to be your accountability partner. It really is better if they commit to the program with you.

Commit to call each other every morning and pray together for your diets. Maybe walk together a few times a week. Share the cooking by having her prepare one recipe and you prepare the other. It really makes a difference when you make this thirty-day commitment with a friend, sister, mother, or spouse.

3. HIS PRINCESS 30-DAY FAST FOR HER KING

We are going to fast off the following foods for thirty days. Before you read the things you are giving up, let me tell you the things you will be receiving in exchange for your fast. You will taste life like never before. Your mind will be renewed as you seek Him every day for strength. You will begin to handle the world around you with a new strength. You will give up guilt from overeating and experience the feeling of being victorious! Remember the prophet Daniel: when he gave up eating the delicacies in the king's palace, God blessed him with favor, wisdom, and strength.

FAST OFF . . . WHITE SUGAR

I have to admit that those sugary treats taste like heaven going down, but they torment our bodies while passing through. Think about what happens to a car when someone puts sugar in the gas tank: it kills the engine. Our bodies react in a similar way.

Believe it or not, sugar should be labeled "legal drug." Our bodies actually go into a state of detoxification when we give this up, with withdrawal symptoms similar to what an alcoholic experiences giving up alcohol. God created the natural form of sugar found in raw fruits, raw vegetables, and honey and molasses. These sweeteners provide fuel for the cells of the body. But man stepped in and "enhanced" God's sugar by using fourteen steps to process sugarcane and sugar beets to make sucrose.

There's an excellent book called *Sugar Blues* by William Dufty (Warner Books). In the next few pages, I'm going to share some things I learned from this book as well as some information I've picked up from the Internet.

> *Bleached white sugar has a toxic, drugging effect on the body. Even in small doses, it causes the immune system's capability to decrease by as much as 50 percent. When it enters the blood- stream, it takes on the forms of carbonic acid, acetic acid, and alcohol. Acetic acid literally burns up our cells.*
>
> Sugar has been known to contribute to depression, fatigue, irritability, hypoglycemia, diabetes, hyperactivity, and violent outrages. A study was done in a mental hospital in which the patients had all bleached white sugar and bleached white flour removed from their diets. Within thirty days, 50 percent of the patients had their mental health restored.
>
> The average American consumes 120 pounds a year of this sweet white stuff, and unfortunately we're usually addicted to sugar as infants before we ever get home from the hospital (bot- tled sugar water is the beverage of choice by hospitals).
>
> The good news is that we can kick the habit. As we wean ourselves from sugary foods and drinks, our taste buds become retrained, and our overindulged cravings for sweets diminish.
>
> (For more research about the effects of sugar, read *Sugar Blues* by William Dufty.)

This will be hard at first but worth the withdrawals. You will taste life in a whole new way. There are some wonderful sugar replacements found in the recipes in the His Princess Meal Plan & Recipes section of this book.

Fast Off . . . All Artificial Sweeteners

Somehow we've bought the lie that artificial sweeteners are safe and a better alternative to sugar. Artificial sweeteners are, well, artificial. There are studies that show the kinds of damage they can do, but even if you don't believe those studies, think about moving away from artificial substances. At least try that for thirty days and see if you don't feel better. This artificial "guilt-free fix" is affecting an enormous number of people without their knowledge. The food fact is that if we're going to eat like a true Princess of the Lord, we're going to stop eating fake food that our Father in heaven did not make.

Fast Off . . . Fake Food

> *When you sit to dine with a ruler,*
>   *note well what is before you,*
> *and put a knife to your throat*
>   *if you are given to gluttony.*
> *Do not crave his delicacies,*
>   *for that food is deceptive.*
>
> *Proverbs 23:1–3*

"Do not be deceived: God cannot be mocked. A man reaps what he sows" (Galatians 6:7). We are certainly reaping the effects of poor nutrition, lack of exercise, sleep deprivation, and ignorance.

The food industry makes billions of dollars each year off of our ignorance. Somehow, their marketing magic has made us feel safe eating foods labeled *fat free, sugar free,* and *artificial flavor.* How safe are we? I have learned over the years that most of the artificially enhanced, beautifully packaged, overprocessed foods we buy aren't really even food at all. In some cases, the packaging would be safer to eat than the food inside. *Fast food* is a perfect title, because it's better to fast than to eat it. Let's go back to the beginning and eat from the garden our Father in heaven grew for His girls!

Fast Off . . . White Flour

Do you know what our food manufacturers are doing with our pasty white flour? It's time to swallow another food fact, so get ready.

First, they take beautiful brown whole grain designed by God to nourish and flourish our bodies, and they remove all the wheat germ and bran. Then they bleach it white with chemicals similar to Clorox bleach. To add insult to injury, they then sell the wheat germ and bran back to us and call it health food.

Check the package when you buy your flour. Unless the label states "unbleached," I'm sad to say that you'll be ingesting bleach with your bread. So read the labels, get rid of the chemicals, and get ready to eat for excellence!

Fast Off . . . White Potato, White Rice, and Corn

When you are wanting to break food addictions and lose weight, it is best to give up what I call "white food." Corn, potatoes, and rice are carbohydrates that turn into sugar very fast in our bodies, and they tend to make us tired and overweight. Unless you're a runner who runs ten to twenty miles a week, it is for your benefit to stick to all raw fruits, vegetables, lean meats, and low-fat complex carbohydrates. *(See the meal plan and recipes section.)*

FAST OFF . . . BUYING FOODS YOU CAN'T EAT

The first step to detoxifying your body is to throw away everything in your kitchen cupboards and refrigerator that is fake food. White sugar, bleached white flour, soft drinks. Don't say you don't want to waste money by getting rid of so much food. *It will cost much more to buy back your health if you continue to eat this toxic food.*

If you have a family, don't announce out loud that you're throwing away their goodies. This could be more hazardous to your health than the toxic food. Slowly begin to introduce more fresh foods into the meals. If you have dessert recipes they love, then switch the white flour to organic spelt and/or brown rice flour. Switch the white sugar to birch sugar or honey, and adjust accordingly for substitutions. Remember, this is *not* a diet—it's a new way of life.

We spend years trashing our bodies, but the good news is that it takes only five to thirty days to start to reverse the curse, depending on how severe the internal damage is. For some, that detoxification time can feel like an eternity.

You may experience headaches and flulike symptoms; to speed up the detoxification process, increase your water and fiber intake. After the toxins are removed, you will experience a euphoric feeling of wellness unlike anything you've ever known. The whites of your eyes will be whiter, your skin will glow, your mind will feel clear, your energy level will increase, and you'll begin to enjoy life the way God intended you to.

FAST AFTER 7:00 P.M.

This is the best health and weight-loss secret I have ever discovered. Basically you are giving your body a break for ten to twelve hours a day. This will shrink your stomach and help you to sleep better. Sometimes I feel a little low-blood-sugar headache coming on, so I do always keep a hard-boiled egg in my fridge. I combine it with a sliced-up apple, and that makes a good snack if you really need something.

His Princess Exercise Plan

EXERCISE 20–30 MINUTES 5 TIMES PER WEEK

We can live forty days without food, four days without water, but we will die in four minutes without oxygen. When God made man, He put in him a breath of life for him to exist. In the Garden of Eden, God blew the breath of life into Adam's nose. Some of us desperately need to learn to breathe deep. Exercise is essential to get oxygen to your cells. God created us to be physically active.

Oxygen brings life to our bodies.

Oxygen . . . detoxifies our blood.

Oxygen . . . strengthens our immune system.

Oxygen . . . heightens concentration and alertness.

Oxygen . . . rejuvenates and revitalizes unhealthy cells.

Oxygen . . . slows down the aging process.

Oxygen . . . helps fight depression.

Not only does oxygen help your body burn fat, it is the very essence of life. So give yourself the gift of exercise. You deserve to take a twenty-to-thirty-minute break for you to refresh your mind and body with some exercise.

Worship While You Work Out

There are many ways to exercise our bodies. My favorite is prayer walks, and if the weather does not permit, I have an exercise cardio machine that I use. I turn up my Christian praise music and sing to the Lord while I refresh my body. Aerobics classes and/or videos are great as well. Whatever you do to honor your King by exercising, make it about Him and think about the wonderful benefits and blessing your body is receiving.

His Princess Beauty Rest & Hydrating Plan

HYDRATE YOUR BODY BY DRINKING PURE WATER

Bless your body first thing in the morning by drinking a huge glass of purified water on an empty stomach. I realize the water doesn't smell like your coffee, but it's a sweet aroma to your body's engine. Water puts oxygen into your blood, and the blood brings oxygen to your brain. It cleans out your colon, flushes out fat, relieves water retention, creates beautiful skin, gives you more energy, removes toxins from your body, and is essential to your health.

Our bodies require a minimum of six to eight glasses of purified water (not tap water, which usually contains chlorine and other toxins) per day.

Sadly our coffee, tea, or sodas actually dehydrate us. Most people only drink one to two glasses of water per day. Believe it or not, as a nation we actually consume more soft drinks than we do water. Just remember, when you wake up, start drinking and continue drinking throughout the day. You will begin to feel so alive inside. (Be sure to look at the Royally Refreshing Drinks recipes in the last section.)

HIS PRINCESS BEAUTY REST

Rest is not only crucial to our health and attitudes toward life, it is a command from our King. It is one of the Ten Commandments.

Our Daddy in heaven wants His girls rested so they can be effective. Rest means take a vacation from all your chores once a week. Rest is a gift from our God. He is giving you permission to take a day for you and rest in Him. I promise if you will obey your Father's rules about the Sabbath, He will restore the time you think you have lost and multiply the work of your hands the following day.

Remember, the next thirty days is about honoring our God with our bodies in every way—rest, exercise, and healthy diet. Wow, are you going to feel amazing next month! You will probably find this as your new way of life, and thirty days will turn into a vibrant life of victory and vitality for you to enjoy all of your days.

WORDS OF ENCOURAGEMENT BEFORE WE START

Blowing it. If you do blow it at one meal, one of the worst things you can do is condemn yourself over and over again. Make a point not to stress out about it. Just get back on track at the next meal.

Don't weigh yourself. A scale should not be your motivation. Remember, you are doing this for God's glory!

Remember it's worth it! The time and energy it takes to eat healthy and exercise is well worth every minute. Be strong in the Lord's strength, do your very best, and God will do the rest.

No food tastes as good as being healthy feels.

His Princess Love Letter

My Princess,

Your body is so special to Me. I carefully created every part of you. You truly are fearfully and wonderfully made. I made you in My image, and I love you. I don't want you to waste another day worrying about what you don't look like or how much you weigh.

Come to Me in the morning and let Me be your mirror. Let Me design your diet; let Me be the strength you need to become your healthiest. You don't have to do this alone; I am here to give you all you need to be free and at peace with yourself.

Love,
Your King, your Identity

His Princess
Daily Devotions

I praise you because I am fearfully and wonderfully
made;
your works are wonderful,
I know that full well.

Psalm 139:14

Day 1

The Diet War Begins . . .
Take Your Royal Position

Then the LORD God said to the woman, "What is this you have done?" The woman said, "The serpent deceived me, and I ate."

Genesis 3:13

I've been sixty pounds overweight—and I've won the crown of Mrs. United States of America. I have been called the "Fat Girl" in high school who never had a prom date—and I have appeared on the cover of a fitness magazine. I've been in bondage to bulimia and free from food controlling my life. But no matter what season I'm in regarding my health and weight, I've discovered I am not alone.

As much as I would like to leave this battle with food behind me, I can't in all good conscience do so, because I have discovered that too many of God's chosen daughters are facing the same struggles. They are in one of three places when it comes to their bodies and self-image:

1. FOOD OBSESSION/ADDICTION

We feel like we can't control ourselves because our food cravings are controlling us. We have given up on the hope of ever losing weight. To make matters worse, we emotionally beat ourselves up with guilt and regret for what we ate that day, and we allow our weight to measure our worth. This food obsession keeps us from becoming the best version of ourselves.

2. "Barbie Bondage"

We are always on a diet and exercising our bodies, yet somehow we are never at peace with our image or our weight, and no amount of shopping, new hairstyles, or weight loss can make us feel good about ourselves. I call this the "Barbie Bondage Syndrome"—perfected on the outside and empty, depressed souls on the inside.

3. Eating Disorders

Tragically, millions of girls and women (Christian or not) battle with an eating disorder of some kind and are destroying their bodies daily.

WHY? Because we have bought the lie that who God created us to be is not good enough, so we bow down to a man-made golden idol of airbrushed perfection and abuse our bodies to become something that is unobtainable.

I can't help but wonder if the first fall of man, which was between a woman and food, is why we women have been struggling with this food issue and our body image ever since. Was it that first act of disobedience that birthed this battle with the way we women see ourselves . . . how we measure our worth? Prior to the fall the woman was not aware of her body; however, after the fall she felt shame for the first time.

The truth is, our Daddy in heaven—*the King above all kings*—has chosen our bodies as His dwelling place. The time is now to fight for our freedom and to learn to treasure our temples to bring glory to our King, not to ourselves. If you're ready to lose weight once and for all, regain your health and energy, and become the best version of you, then let's get to the heart of the matter and make every calorie count for Christ.

His Princess Prayer for You

Dear Lord,

I ask today that You would open my sister's eyes and heart to the freedom You hold for her. Let her see that it is a gift, a special treasure, that she will receive as she learns to look to You to be her mirror and to see whatever keeps her from fully experiencing You, Lord God. We claim victory in the name of Jesus today, Lord! Prove Your power through her as she commits these next thirty days to You, Lord, and lead her to complete freedom from food ever controlling her again!

In Jesus' name I pray, Amen

"You will seek me and find me when you seek me with all your heart. I will be found by you," declares the LORD, "and will bring you back from captivity."

Jeremiah 29:13–14

His Princess in Action

Every time you're tempted to break your fast, say out loud to yourself, *"No food tastes as good as being healthy feels."*

Treasure of Truth for Today

Diet is *not* about Denial . . . it's about Desire.

Day 2

Barbie Bondage

Wherever your treasure is, there your heart and thoughts will also be.

Matthew 6:21 NLT[1]

 want to confess to you up front that my body image becomes an internal battle for me when I allow my self-worth to be measured by the idols of this world. So to keep us free from Barbie Bondage and get our focus on our King, we will have to get our hearts right and our minds fixed on eternity.

If we were to be brutally honest with ourselves, we would probably have to admit that most of our efforts to lose weight have been motivated by a desire to glorify ourselves. Rarely, if ever, do we look at a weight-loss plan and think of our Lord and King and the royal call He has on our lives. If you think about it, most of us will do whatever it takes to attract a man or look good at a reunion or wedding. We will also lose weight to win people's approval and get their attention. But why can't we approach our diets primarily as a way of honoring the One who created our bodies? The truth is, we are more effective in our witness to the world when we feel healthy and are in control of our diets.

Before I became a Christian, I lost sixty pounds in order to compete for a worldly crown. All I ever thought about was me, and the scale dictated my day. I was willing to go without any food I craved and to spend countless hours exercising so I could look my best. I spent five intense years training, and I was totally committed to getting what I wanted more than anything—a national crown awarded by man. When I finally won that crown, most would think "mission accomplished." However, as I look back on those years, I realize the reason I could never stay fit for life: my heart was selfish, my goals were all about me, and I was striving after those goals in my own strength.

Today I no longer search for a crown appointed by man. I have been given the greatest crown of all, the crown of life appointed by God. A crown that gives me something the world can never give—peace. My life makes sense. God now uses my pain for a purpose: to bless and encourage others. I have a renewed passion for people and a God-given power to live out my passions and let go of the pains from my past. My past no longer torments me. Instead, I have learned a valuable lesson about life—that it is not about me. It is about God and others!

His Princess Prayer

Dear Lord,

Please forgive me for trying to bring glory to myself. You are the only one who should get the glory and honor in my life. I need to confess that I can't change the way I am alone. I need You to reach down from heaven and rearrange my heart,

my mind, and my life. I am so blessed to have a
Father in heaven who is only a prayer away!
In Jesus' name I ask these things, Amen

His Princess in Action

Pray for one thing you can do this week to add to someone's life in word or deed. It will help keep the focus off you and put it back onto your purpose.

Treasure of Truth for Today

Who we are is found in . . .
Our character . . . not our appearance
Our choices . . . not our possessions
Our courage . . . not our comfort
Our compassion . . . not our successes

Day 3

Break the Bondage

How foolish are those who manufacture idols.
These prized objects are really worthless.
The people who worship idols don't know this,
*   so they are all put to shame.*

Isaiah 44:9 NLT[2]

hen I first set out to lose weight as a teenager, my stepmom Susie taught me how to eat healthy, take care of my body, and exercise moderately. By following her instructions, I lost all my extra weight, regained my health and energy, and enjoyed the benefits of a healthy lifestyle for almost four years.

It wasn't until I was sitting at a modeling audition watching three beautiful, thin young girls eating several candy bars at a time that my problems began. As I sat there and watched these three young ladies obviously enjoying themselves, it drove me crazy. I couldn't stand not knowing. "How can you possibly eat all that candy and stay so thin?" I blurted out.

They looked back at me as they fumbled with handfuls of wrappers, their cheeks so stuffed they could hardly speak.

"Easy," they mumbled. "We just go to the bathroom and throw it up!"

Ooooh, yuck! I thought. *How disgusting!*

A few weeks later, I made the mistake of stuffing myself at a dinner. Afterward, a strange fear gripped me as an old, familiar thought popped into my head: *Sheri Rose, look what you did! You just ate like a pig, and now you're going to be fat again!*

That fear gave me the impulse to go to the bathroom and try something that, just a few days before, was unthinkable. *After all, those beautiful, thin models did it,* I thought. *Just this once . . . I've got to get this food out of my body!* I had no idea that "just this once" was going to turn into a life-threatening habit.

From that day on, every meal became a mental battle—a desperate, private struggle between my desire to be thin and the pleasure of eating. *Should I eat right, or should I eat what I want and just throw it up?*

As I entered into this bulimic lifestyle, I learned there were other tricks to control my weight. I began using laxatives and water pills and exercising compulsively. I hopped nervously onto the scale at least five times a day to make sure I wasn't putting on any extra pounds. I was so obsessed with my body that I couldn't concentrate on any other area of my life.

I knew I was in bondage, but I was afraid to tell anybody what I was doing to myself, fearful that others would see me as a failure. I tried with all my strength and willpower to control my unhealthy, compulsive-eating behavior, but the harder I tried to break out of this bondage, the more bound I became.

I felt as if I were doomed to be locked up forever in this private prison. People gladly accepted me outwardly, but if they could see me behind closed doors, they would find that I felt like a total failure. What started out as a quick and easy weight-loss strategy ended up rotting my teeth, damaging my kidneys, and weakening my heart. Every part of my body suffered pain in this disastrous, personal hell. Of all the poor choices I have ever made, this has been the one I regret the most. It's embarrassing, it's scary, it's lonely, and it's hard to find help. It's a private sin from which only God Himself can deliver you.

Gratefully, God has healed me of this terrible eating disorder. But once you have opened the door to sin, it can tempt you again. I used to think that once I prayed for God to heal me, I would never have to battle with bulimia again. I've grown up a lot since then.

Paul, in his letter to the church in Rome, describes the battle between the flesh and the spirit within us. While we may have every intention of doing the right thing, sometimes we fall prisoner to the sinful nature within us. Paul cried out to be rescued from this bondage and found that Jesus Christ was there to rescue him without condemning him (see Romans 7–8).

God freed me from the bondage of bulimia. But the key to my deliverance from bulimia was not just in a prayer but also in *taking the necessary steps to walk in the Spirit and seal the deliverance!* Once I realized that these airbrushed photos were the very thing that was keeping me from liking the way God created me, I fasted off beauty magazines and began to allow the Lord to define my worth.

When God delivers you out of bondage, He always directs you somewhere better!

His Princess Prayer

Dear God,
*   Please forgive me for worshiping the man-made*
idols of this world, for allowing them to determine

*my worth. I kneel here at Your feet and lay down
the lies I have believed, and I choose on this day to
believe that I am who You say I am. Please help me
to look to You as my mirror. Guard my mind from
ever believing the lies of man over Your truth, and
help me to walk in Your confidence, not my own.
Thank You that I do not have to win Your love and
affection for me. What a privilege it is to be Your
Princess!*

    In Jesus' name I pray, Amen

His Princess in Action

Write down on a piece of scrap paper a lie that you have believed about yourself, then walk over to a trash can and throw it away.

Treasure of Truth for Today

You are a treasured daughter of the Highest King!
Don't allow any worthless idols to determine your worth
or cause you to believe lies about yourself.

Overweight, Depressed, and Tired

Now the serpent was more crafty than any of the wild animals the LORD God had made. He said to the woman, "Did God really say, 'You must not eat from any tree in the garden'?"

Genesis 3:1

A friend of mine recently interviewed with a national Fortune 500 pharmaceutical company. She happened to have some literature from my teaching on spiritual, relational, emotional, and physical health and showed it to one of the executives from the company. He took one look at it and tossed it down with a smirk. "This program better not work, or we'll go broke! We make millions off of women who are overweight, depressed, and tired."

I used to travel through life in two gears: park and fifth. I pushed myself to the highest speed limits possible, ignoring the big yellow warning lights telling me, "Slow down! Rest! Severe exhaustion ahead."

I was so consumed with getting to my destination of the day, completing my unrealistic to-do list, that I didn't hear my body's cry for wellness. I was living life in fast-forward, and when I didn't think I could handle traveling one more mile at this speed, I pushed down the pedal even harder. I thought the

Scripture that says "The spirit is willing but the flesh is weak" meant it's okay and even spiritual to ignore your body's need for rest, replenishment, relaxation, and restoration.

The next thing I knew, I experienced a crash and was thrown out onto the road of reality. There I was, speaking to a group of ladies on spiritual excellence, when I collapsed onto the floor. This was not a spiritual experience; I mean, I totally blacked out. That evening I was taken to the hospital and was diagnosed with Epstein-Barr virus, which operates like chronic fatigue syndrome. My immune system had completely shut down, and I was so exhausted I couldn't lift my head off the pillow. The doctor told me I would have to stop all activity. Shut down. In other words, pull my lifestyle out of fifth gear and put it in park, indefinitely. There I lay, face-to-face with the fear that I might never regain my health and energy. It wasn't until I stopped eating junk food and repented to the Lord for trashing His temple that He healed me, and within four weeks of obedience, God completely healed my body.

Interestingly, today we see that every study done in the last thirty years on diet, health, and disease prevention points without fail to the same time-tested diet written thousands of years ago by the God who created our bodies. Obviously, we can see that our Father in heaven knows what is best for His daughters to eat.

His Princess Prayer

Dear God,

I am sick and tired of being sick or tired all the time. I give You permission to convict me of the things I am doing that drain me and don't bring glory to You. Give me the wisdom on when to say YES when You want me to commit to something and the strength to say NO when I need rest. I am ready to take a spiritual vacation from my overcommitted, stressed life and enter into a time of rest for my soul.

In Jesus' name, Amen

His Princess in Action

Treat yourself to a fifteen-minute nap every day this week and go to bed by 10 p.m. at the latest. You will be more effective rested!

Come to me, all you who are weary and burdened, and I will give you rest.

Matthew 11:28

Treasure of Truth for Today

If the devil can't make you bad,
his next trick is to make you busy.

Day 5

God's Temple or
Our Trash Can

*The thief's purpose is to steal and kill and destroy. My purpose
is to give them a rich and satisfying life.*

John 10:10 NLT[2]

ur God gives us a warning: Satan comes to steal, kill,
and destroy . . .

And if we continue to make God's temple our trash
can, we are helping the devil accomplish his mission—one meal
at a time.

I've discovered that whenever you ask a woman how she is
doing, you will probably get one of four answers: "I'm so tired!"
"I'm so bloated!" "I'm so sick!" or "I'm so-o-o-o fat!" Then we
get together in a group while we're munching on cakes, candy,
coffee, and chips, and we talk on and on about how sick, tired,
and fat we are! What is wrong with this picture?

After trashing our bodies, we drop to our knees, bow our
heads, and beg God to help us not to feel sick. We know that
we need healing and that God can heal us, but we make His
temple our trash can! It's like drinking a bottle of whiskey
before coming to church and praying to God to help us not
feel drunk.

Honestly, the reason I can talk so freely about this subject is because, well, I am a food addict. The only thing I love doing more than talking is eating. One of my greatest joys in life is food. When I'm celebrating, I eat. When I'm tired, I eat. When I'm sad, I eat. When I'm anxious, I eat. When I'm in pain, I eat. I have spent years running to the refrigerator for refuge. And when I get hungry, my personality actually changes—from Dr. Jekyll to Mr. Hyde! While others may snack off-and-on all day long, I actually prefer eating only one meal a day—it starts in the morning and ends when I fall asleep.

In the past, when at a restaurant, I used to eat until I was completely bloated and then tackle the waiter for the dessert menu. When weddings took too long, I would get irritated because I couldn't wait to get to the reception to eat. I've been known to push people out of line so I could get the corner piece of cake that has the most icing. Of all the obstacles in my life, my addiction to food has been the most difficult for me to overcome. I've only come up with one good reason not to honor God by eating healthy:

What would I talk about if I felt good?
Being bloated, sick, and tired are very popular topics of conversation.

Does God really care how much we eat? That question is clearly answered in Proverbs: "When you sit to dine . . . note well what is before you, and put a knife to your throat if you are given to gluttony" (Proverbs 23:1–2).

It's time to face the truth that overeating is gluttony. And gluttony is sin! Because of my love for food and my tendency to overeat, I make an effort not to bring foods into my home that will be tempting. Just as an alcoholic breaking an addiction doesn't stock his cabinets with alcoholic beverages, I don't stock my cabinets with tempting food and then try in my own strength not to overeat. At first, these changes were a little hard on my family because they loved junk food as much as I did. But I was honest with them about my addiction, and they agreed to help me by not bringing tempting foods home. Besides, they know that "if Mom isn't happy—no one's happy!"

Let's rejoice that we are breaking free from food ever controlling our lives again. From this day forward we will eat like a daughter of the King and be satisfied!

His Princess Prayer

Dear Lord,

I admit that many times I run to food for comfort instead of running to You, my true comfort and place of peace. Remind me when I am tempted to stuff my body with food to instead fill myself up with Your bread of life in Your Word. I am sorry, God, for every time I've made my menu more meaningful than Your love for me. I need Your help in this area and ask now for Your tender touch.

In Jesus' name, Amen

His Princess in Action

Try eating all your meals this week on a salad plate instead of a dinner plate, and don't go back for a second helping of food.

Treasure of Truth for Today

You are a treasured Princess of the Lord.
His love is what will really satisfy your cravings.

A Touch from the Savior

"If I just touch his clothes, I will be healed." Immediately her
bleeding stopped and she felt in her body that she was freed from
her suffering.

Mark 5:29

In the fifth chapter of the Gospel of Mark, there's an example of a woman who knew exactly to whom to turn
in time of trouble. This example of physical suffering
and the steps that brought her healing apply to the emotional
pain you may be experiencing today.

She knew she needed healing.

The bleeding this poor woman experienced could not be
hidden. For twelve years she was ceremonially unclean, and
everything and everyone she touched each day was made unclean. She was way past the stage of "this suffering I feel is no
big deal." She had obviously confessed her need and reached a
point of desperation. If you're going to move out of denial and
get real with God, face your need head-on and move beyond
suppression to *confession.*

She tried everything else.

The Bible says that not only was this woman victimized by
this ailment for twelve years, but she literally spent all that she
had on professional remedies—only to discover that she was

getting worse! Do you need to acknowledge that your own efforts and worldly treatments are just not going to be strong enough to heal you? Perhaps you haven't exhausted all of your human effort. This poor woman had to wait twelve years before she had the chance of a lifetime for healing. It took her twelve years to "take hold" of Jesus. How long will it take you?

She didn't care what people thought.

When you want to get healed badly enough, you'll "fight the crowds" to pursue it. If, for example, you had a physical ailment like severe chest pains, you would tell someone right away, wouldn't you? Of course you would. But most people, even in churches, are too embarrassed or ashamed to seek help for emotional suffering. In the Gospel of Mark, the suffering woman wasn't just in physical pain. She must have felt deep emotional pain as well. Because she was "unclean" according to the Law, she was literally a social outcast from her friends and family and from worshiping in the temple. The pain her spirit felt from rejection must have been unbearable. Yet, do you think any embarrassment or pride or condemnation from others was going to keep her away from her Healer? The crowd was pressing in around Jesus from all sides. There was a frenzied stampede of Jesus fans. But one frail, wounded lady let nothing stop her. What is keeping you from your Healer today?

She discovered acceptance and understanding of her frailty and experienced the power of Jesus.

"If I could just touch the hem of His garment, I would be healed." What faith she had! She had no more money. She had no more friends. She had no more strength. She had no more answers. She had no more self-confidence. But with faith . . . she had no more obstacles!

Jesus knows and understands your pain, and He accepts you in your frail condition. When your little bit of faith lays hold of

the power of Jesus, He is able to grant you peace and freedom—
and, in His time, healing.

His Princess Love Letter

Dear Princess,

I will always be with you in sickness and in health.
Call out to Me, My Princess. Let Me, your Lord, comfort you and take you to a place where your soul can
be at rest even when your body is ill. I will provide
peace and healing for My girl. You have nothing to
fear, My beloved. I was there when you took your
first breath, and I will be there when you take your
last. I can heal you with just a touch, or I can carry
you home to heaven with me. Just know I will hold
you now and until we finally see one another face-
to-face.

Love,
Your Prince and Healer

His Princess in Action

Cry out to your Lord right now and you will feel Him touch you by His Spirit as you read the love letter below:

> The LORD is my shepherd;
>   I have all that I need.
> He lets me rest in green meadows;
>   he leads me beside peaceful streams.
> He renews my strength.
>
> Psalm 23:1–3 NLT[2]

Treasure of Truth for Today

His touch . . . is medicine for our souls.

Day 7

Is Your Body Talking to You?

Therefore, I urge you, brothers, in view of God's mercy, to offer your bodies as living sacrifices, holy and pleasing to God—this is your spiritual act of worship. Do not conform any longer to the pattern of this world, but be transformed by the renewing of your mind.

Romans 12:1–2

If you're like me, you've probably tried everything possible to find enough energy to make it through the day. Coffee, sugar, vitamin pep pills—there's plenty of artificial and natural stimulants to choose from, but the problem is that our adrenal glands will soon burn out and our entire immune system ends up broken down. When this happens, sickness and disease eventually win in our battle for health and energy.

Don't look to a substance to keep you healthy; listen to your body. God put a quiet voice inside of us that starts with a whisper and gets louder the longer we ignore it. It starts with physical discomfort like headaches, indigestion, and a need for rest. If we do not listen, our body talks louder by communicating through sicknesses and severe exhaustion. If we continue to ignore it, it screams, "Breakdown! I can't take any more!" Is your body talking to you?

Ask yourself the following questions:

- Does your body wake up refreshed or exhausted?
- Does your body have energy throughout the day?
- How does your body feel after you eat a meal?
- Do you have trouble getting a good night's sleep?
- Does your body feel achy or in pain often?
- Do you suffer from headaches often?
- Do you have digestive problems?
- Do you have allergy symptoms such as a runny nose or puffy eyes?

When you experience any of these things, your body is talking to you. It's telling you, "Something is not right. Please help me!" These symptoms are not normal. They're your body trying to get rid of the toxins you have been putting inside of it. THESE ARE WARNING SIGNS! The tragedy is that most of us don't take the warning signs seriously. We justify them by making excuses until one day it's too late to turn back. If you're sick and tired of being sick and tired, you're going to have to do more than complain about it or try to drug yourself back to health. You must begin eating for excellence.

God desires us to be in good health. Third John 2 says, "Beloved, I pray that in all respects you may prosper and be in good health, just as your soul prospers." The road is wide that leads to destruction. The path to the crown of health is narrow. Don't look to man's shortcuts—look to God's long-term plan for a long, healthy life! He loves you and longs to bless you, but He can't reward disobedience when you make His temple your trash can.

Our society has been programmed into thinking that we can put anything we want into our bodies, abuse our bodies, neglect our bodies, and then when our bodies break down, all we have to do is run to the doctor, who will give us a magic pill. In just a few days, we will be all better.

The truth is, it just doesn't work that way. We need to take responsibility and do our part to take care of God's temple, or we will never experience the blessing of good health.

His Princess Prayer

Dear Lord,

Please help me hear the warning signs You send that tell me I need to make a change in order to honor You with my body. I don't want to abuse my body any longer. I need Your help. Please, Father, show me the way to recovery and restoration that I may walk in good health.

In Jesus' name, Amen

His Princess in Action

Review the questions listed in the devotion and write down the physical ailments you suffer from, then write down some changes you can make to get yourself on the right road to recovery.

Treasure of Truth for Today

We cannot change our past, but it's never too late to change our future by the choices we make today.

Warning: Listen! Your Spirit Is Speaking!

For you are a slave to whatever controls you.

2 Peter 2:1 NLT²

ave you ever been told you're too emotional? Perhaps you have asked yourself, "If God loves me, why am I feeling such pain?" Or maybe you have heard Christians say, "Emotions are ungodly; you need to ignore your feelings and live by faith." Do you wonder why, then, did God give you emotions in the first place, if you are supposed to ignore them?

Women are notorious for beating themselves up with guilt for being "too emotional." We can't understand why we feel the way we do, we're told we shouldn't feel the way we do, and then we convince ourselves that the powerful emotions we're experiencing must stem from some flaw in our character. We then condemn ourselves. What a burden it is to carry that kind of guilt heaped unmercifully on top of our already heavy emotions. If you've been in bondage to this kind of guilt, you can take great comfort in this wonderful truth: it is impossible to be too emotional! Let me assure you that there is nothing wrong with your emotions. Emotions are designed by God for a reason. God does love you. He designed you to feel because you are created in His image—and the almighty God feels! Did you know there are more than two thousand instances in the Bible that refer to the emotions of God?

His Princess Love Letter

Dear Princess,

I long for you to know freedom from guilt and anger, from fear and worry, from hopelessness and purposelessness. I loved you with My life so that you can be free of such things. Nothing in this world—nothing except you yourself, My love—can keep you from walking in My freedom. So come to Me and read My Word. Cry out to Me, My love, and I will give you the keys to living in freedom. You will become My Princess Warrior when you pray and obey My voice. I will never hurt you or leave you alone, so come to Me, My daughter, and I, your Daddy in heaven, will soothe your soul, restore your peace of mind, and set your precious feet on solid ground.

Love,
Your King and your Freedom

It seems obvious why a loving God would create positive emotions like joyfulness, peacefulness, excitement, and confidence, but why would unpleasant and negative emotions like loneliness, grief, rejection, despair, anger, and frustration be a part of His creative plan for us? Can we assume that they are just part of the curse of sin?

No, they serve a purpose. Take a moment to reflect on a favorite movie. Many times we don't think about it, but the musical score plays a critical role; it adds life, dimension, and vibrant color to each scene. Sometimes its foreboding, ominous theme warns of looming danger. In the next scene it might enhance the beauty of a romantic embrace or reflect the sorrow of love swept away in death. To hit the mute button during a heart-pounding, climactic finish would be a crime!

Emotions, both positive and negative, were created by God to reveal the condition of the human spirit—a warning sign that something needs to be dealt with and given to our King. Just as physical pain reveals that there is something wrong with our body, our emotions are a warning signal that something needs attention in our spirit. God has placed within us warning signs for us to get life right and live in complete freedom.

His Princess in Action

Pray the prayer below, then be still and listen as God helps you recognize the root of your feelings. Then write down what He reveals. Writing it down makes it become real, and it gives you a touchstone for taking the next step toward freedom.

His Princess Prayer

Dear Jesus,

I feel _____(fill in what you feel), *and
I don't want to live in this emotional place any longer.
As frightening as this is for me right now, I pray,
Father God, that You would reveal the root of my
unhealthy actions and reactions. I need You to show
me what is going on inside of me so that I can give my
heart and all of my hurts to You. I want to change,
and I ask You to intervene now and show me what I
need to do to be healed and whole. I am ready to let
You remove the root of my pain. Thank You for being
my safe place, and thank You that I can come to You
with anything. I love You and I praise You for Your
faithfulness to me. Now, by the work of Your Holy
Spirit, please help me.*

In Your name I pray, Amen

Then you will know the truth, and the truth will set you free.

John 8:32

Treasure of Truth for Today

How you feel . . . is not who you are.
Who you are is a chosen Princess of the Lord!

Hopelessness Is Just an Illusion

For the LORD your God is going with you! He will fight for you against your enemies, and he will give you victory!

Deuteronomy 20:4 NLT[1]

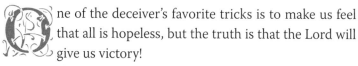ne of the deceiver's favorite tricks is to make us feel that all is hopeless, but the truth is that the Lord will give us victory!

Remember the Israelites? God rescued them and brought them out of slavery in Egypt—and immediately to the edge of the Red Sea. There the chosen, rescued people stood, stuck between what looked like a sea of hopelessness and their enemies charging toward them. I am sure they felt abandoned and defeated, and we know they questioned why God had set them free if they were going to die defeated by their Egyptian enemies. However, it was that hopeless situation that God used to destroy their Egyptian enemies once and for all. And that sea of hopelessness gave God another opportunity to prove His power: He parted the waters and His people walked on dry land to their freedom. Then He closed the waters, and the Israelites watched their enemies die before their very eyes.

Many times life's greatest trials give us greater faith. The Israelites did not have to do anything to see victory except walk to their freedom through the open door their God provided.

God wants to carry you into victory, my Sister Princess! He has an open door for you. I know that your circumstances may seem hopeless, but God has great things in store for you if you will walk in faith.

Here's how I've been praying for you, the reader . . .

His Princess Prayer for You

Dear Lord,

Open my sister's eyes and heart to the freedom You hold for her. Let her see that it is a gift, a special treasure, that she will receive as she learns to let go of worry, guilt, shame, and whatever keeps her from fully experiencing You, Lord God. We claim victory in the name of Jesus today, Lord! Lead her and deliver her through her sea of hopelessness. Prove Your power through her as she commits these next days to You, Lord, and lead her to complete freedom!

In Jesus' name I pray, Amen

His Princess in Action

Whatever your sea of hopelessness is right now, say the words out loud, "He is God and I am not."

Wherever the Spirit of the Lord is, there is freedom.

2 Corinthians 3:1 NLT[2]

Treasure of Truth for Today

I am the LORD All-Powerful. So don't depend on your own power or strength, but on my Spirit.

Zechariah 4:6 CEV

Day 10

Get Real with God

The LORD hears his people when they call to him for help.
He rescues them from all their troubles.

Psalm 34:17 NLT[2]

f you don't deal with your emotional pain, it will deal with you, your loved ones, and your life. Pretending it doesn't exist won't help you get emotionally fit. I pretended for so long that my pain didn't exist that I earned my doctorate degree in denial.

If we deny or stuff these emotions, we will never be emotionally fit. Some of us think that being spiritual requires denying how we really feel.

If we are not honest about our emotions, covering up the warning signals of our spirit, we will slowly die inwardly. God is a God of truth—and only the truth can set you free. I'm not saying that you should tell the whole world all your problems, but I am saying to tell them to God, the mighty Counselor. If you are having trouble identifying what you are really feeling and why it's affecting you, pray and ask God to show you the hidden hurts that need to be healed. Come out of the shadows into His glorious light and be set free to fly!

David cried out to God every time he was hurting, and he is known as "a man after God's own heart." There was nothing

His Princess Love Letter

Dear Princess,

I see how hard you try to handle your heart, and I know you want to live a life without heartache or pain, My love. But I am asking you to take a step closer to Me, your Daddy in heaven who loves and adores you, by crying out to Me rather than trying to be strong in your own strength. I am not expecting you to pretend pain is not real. The truth is, your tears will wash your soul from the inside out. I will heal your broken heart if you will trust Me with all the pieces. I am your deliverer, My Daughter, and your key to true freedom. So cry out to Me.

Love,
Your King

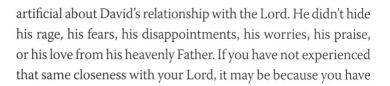

artificial about David's relationship with the Lord. He didn't hide his rage, his fears, his disappointments, his worries, his praise, or his love from his heavenly Father. If you have not experienced that same closeness with your Lord, it may be because you have never known how to let yourself be entirely honest with Him. Don't listen when the enemy whispers that you can save yourself from the pain and problems of this world. When something hurts you or someone angers you, tell your Savior. He died a very real death for you to have access to the throne room of God. He is our place of rest, our safe place. When we are in His presence, He will restore our mind, our body, and our soul. Our Father in heaven wants His daughter to be free! No one loves you more, and no one else has the power or passion for you that your God has. He alone is the only one who can and will heal your heart and soothe your soul. He is the Lover of your soul, and He longs for you to run to Him so that He can heal your every hurt.

If you truly want to be a woman after God's own heart, and want to experience the complete healing God offers you, then run to Him every time you hurt. He is your Daddy in heaven, and He longs to comfort and heal you.

His Princess in Action

It's time to get real with God. Voice to God your bitterness, your jealousy, your envy, your hatred, and your resentment. Many times we tell everybody but God how we feel. Tell Him now; maybe even write a prayer to Him.

Treasure of Truth for Today

Sometimes when we try to handle our pain by ourselves, we are playing our own God. Our Father loves us no matter what emotions we are dealing with. Dying to ourselves does not mean denying ourselves the freedom to deal with what is real.

Adventures with the King

And God is able to make all grace abound to you, so that in all things at all times, having all that you need, you will abound in every good work.

2 Corinthians 9:8

There's nothing more exciting or fulfilling than going on daily adventures with the King. God's Word says that "the steps of a good man [or woman] are ordered by the LORD" (Psalm 37:23 KJV). Did you know that every day your God has an appointment for you to keep? You can, however, miss your divine appointments when you are too busy thinking about your own agenda. If you're not experiencing the joy of your salvation, it may be because you're missing your daily divine appointments!

Divine appointments keep us focused on eternity and give us something exciting to talk about—rather than complaining about the things that challenge and frustrate us during the day.

Because I love to shop, my family says I have a "mall ministry." (I try to convince my husband that my ministry would be much more effective if he'd increase the limit on my shopping budget!) I've had some wonderful divine appointments at the mall. One day while I was shopping for makeup with my sisters-in-law, I noticed that the woman working at the counter was in emotional pain. Even though the counter was full of customers, I pulled her aside, asked her if she was okay, and asked if I could pray for her. She immediately burst into tears. She told me how her husband had just had an affair and had left her and the children. She was devastated, and she didn't know the Lord. After I prayed with her, I asked her if my husband and I could come by her house on Sunday and bring her and her children to church. She said she'd never been to church before, but she was hurting so badly that she was willing to try anything. The pastor gave a message on how God is a father to the fatherless and a husband to the husbandless. With tears in her eyes, the woman came forward with her children; they all gave their lives to Jesus Christ.

Every one of us has the opportunity to be God's extended hand of love to someone in need. The key is to look for the divine appointment that God has scheduled for you each day—and not to be so consumed with your own agenda that you miss the opportunity to touch a life.

God sets up divine interventions just to bless us! When we are looking for our daily divine appointments, we find more than the excitement of being used by God. When we walk in the Spirit, we will find that God has preordained people to cross our path to be a blessing to us as well. There is no greater nourishment for our souls than to know that we are used by God in the midst of our daily life.

His Princess Prayer

Dear Abba Father,

Wipe away my tears once again. Lord, help me to trust You and cry out to You. Even though I cannot see You, I am taking a step of faith and giving You all my fears, tears, and disappointments. Release me and help me cry out to You so I can be free as You love me back to life again.

I pray in Jesus' name, Amen

Love,

Your Daughter who longs to be healed and held by You

His Princess in Action

Write your Prince Jesus a letter pouring out whatever has been locked up inside of you. Then watch and see how relieved you feel when you place your pain in the hands of the Lord who gave His life for your freedom.

Keep in mind that many times it seems more painful as pain is being released than it felt to keep it inside. However, it is truth and tears that set us free to become the women we desire to be, the women God has destined us to be.

Treasure of Truth for Today

His reflection in us is more beautiful
than we could ever make ourselves.

Eliminate the Enemy's Weapons

I am come that they might have life, and that they might have it more abundantly.

John 10:10 KJV

If a police officer came to your door and warned you that your neighbors had just been robbed and killed, you would be on the lookout for anything that could let that enemy in your home or near your loved ones. Our King warns us in His Word that there is an enemy after us who is out to kill, steal, and destroy (John 10:10). He also warns us that if we are not careful, we will help him (the devil) accomplish his mission by what we read, watch, and listen to; we will let him destroy our values, our minds, and our children through the modern entertainment we allow in our homes. Instead, we should be seeking how to make our lives become louder than the world's influence.

I have had the privilege of meeting people from all walks of life: people with fame and fortune; people who are lost and lonely; people who are intellectual, interesting, and intriguing; people who are powerful; and people who are beautiful. But no matter where I have walked in life, I have found a common goal existing in every heart—the search for fulfillment and peace of mind.

Our souls long for internal peace—the peace that is only found in God.

That peace can't be found in beauty magazines or on the television screen. If we are not careful, we will allow the enemy to steal our peace and joy by what we watch and read and listen to.

We are Princess Warriors of the King and have been given the power and privilege to live a better life. Our Father knows what's best for His daughters. His rules and warnings are for our good; they are the key to true freedom from depression, confusion, and destruction. It is not that our King does not want His daughters to have any fun or entertainment; He wants to protect our minds, our bodies, and our souls from destruction. (If you don't believe this is true, take a good look at the fearful, negative, and depressed people who have traded their passion for life and peace of mind for a moment's pleasure.)

Let's get rid of the things that keep us from the abundant life our Savior gave His life for!

His Princess Prayer

Dear Lord,

Show me by Your Holy Spirit what I am watching, reading, or listening to that needs to be eliminated from my mind. I want to have a mind that is focused on You and a heart that is at peace.

In Jesus' name, Amen

His Princess in Action

Fast off all TV and beauty magazines for the next week and see if your mind begins to think clearer, if your heart is happier, and if your spirit has more peace. You may see the world around you in a whole new light.

Treasure of Truth for Today

The devil does not have to destroy us to win.
All he has to do is steal our worth by teaching us lies
about ourselves, and then he has won.

Day 13

Your Shame Is Gone

For the LORD God is our sun and shield.
  He gives us grace and glory.
The LORD withhold no good thing
  from those who do what is right.

Psalm 84:11 NLT²

Many of us overeat because we deal with shame. There is a way out from under the shame and hurt that many of us feel today. When Adam and Eve ate the fruit of the tree, their sin left them with an emotional burden called *shame*. What did Adam do when the voice of his spirit cried out from this strange new emotional pain? He ran and hid himself from God.

When Jesus, the second Adam, hung crucified on the tree, our sin left Him with an emotional burden called *shame*. What did Jesus do when His spirit cried out from this undeserved emotional pain? He willingly bore the pain of our sorrow, our grief, our shame, and our sin . . . yet He opened not His mouth in defense.

If you feel lonely and rejected, or fearful and ashamed, what do you do with your emotional pain? You may have been afflicted by the unloving blows of another person or maybe by your own disobedience.

Whatever the cause, you don't have to feel guilty for crying out to God. When you do cry out, you are identifying with Jesus. You are learning to know Him and the fellowship of His suffering. But when you hide out, you are identifying with Adam and separating yourself from the sweet fellowship of God.

The pain Jesus felt brought us eternal healing and restoration. His suffering brought us into fellowship. God wants us to experience that fellowship by sharing our pain with Him and with other believers. The result is unity, restoration, strength, and yes, healing.

Just remember: the same resurrection power that raised Jesus from the dead will give you the power to deal with your pain and lead you to a more intimate relationship with Him! You'll be able to experience excellence in your life in a way you could never have dreamed possible.

There is no easy way to deal with emotional pain, but God promises that those who sow in tears will reap with joy. The same is true for you. It's time to walk out of the pit of shame and into the promise of God's deliverance and healing.

His Princess Prayer

Dear Lord,

I don't want to hide anymore. Please replace my shame with Your truth. Help me to walk away from what was and run to You. I want to be free from shame once and for all and to clothe myself in Your righteousness and mercy. Cover me now and let me

feel Your Spirit holding me while I begin to allow
You to heal me.
  In Jesus' name I pray, Amen

His Princess in Action

Whatever shame you are dealing with, write it down, then throw it in the trash, saying out loud the words of Jesus on that cross: "It is finished."

Forget the former things;
  do not dwell on the past.
See, I am doing a new thing!
  Now it springs up; do you not perceive it?
I am making a way in the desert
  and streams in the wasteland.

  Isaiah 43:18–19

Treasure of Truth for Today

Your past is not your future . . . You are a new creation.

Day 14

Toxic Love

Love is patient and kind. Love is not jealous or boastful or proud or rude. It does not demand its own way. It is not irritable, and it keeps no record of being wronged.

1 Corinthians 13:4–5 NLT[2]

o you have a spouse, a friend, or a parent who says he or she loves you . . . but you don't understand why this love hurts so badly? If so, you may be experiencing toxic love. Have you ever taken a big bite out of a plum you thought was ripe and winced at the sour taste? Every cell in your mouth screamed out in defense, "Spit it out before you get sick!"

Our bodies were designed to warn us of potentially harmful things, like unripe fruit, in order to keep us from getting sick. In the same way, we recognize whether someone is led by the Spirit by how healthy the "fruit" is in his or her life. Healthy love is a natural product—or fruit—of the Spirit living inside us. "But the fruit of the Spirit is love" (Galatians 5:22).

It may be difficult for you to understand the difference between healthy love and toxic love. If you have only experienced toxic love, how can you even know what healthy love "looks" like? You must learn to recognize the warning signals of a love that is unripe or toxic. Toxic love will make your heart sick; healthy love will make your heart soar.

Responding to Toxic Love Relationships

One of the best examples in the Bible of how we should respond to toxic love is found in the life of Joseph. He went through amazing trials in his life, and they all stemmed from his brothers' jealousy of him. First, they threw him in a pit with plans to kill him. They then sold him into slavery and told their dad that his favorite son was killed by a wild animal. Joseph then wound up in prison after being framed by his boss's wife. He finally got out of prison after two years because he interpreted the Pharaoh's dreams; he eventually rose to power in Egypt as Pharaoh's right-hand man. He even became a huge hero in the land by rescuing millions from a seven-year famine. The story really gets interesting, however, when we see how Joseph responds to his brothers when they come to Egypt for food. Here are some key steps I found from Joseph's response to his brothers' toxic love.

He Didn't Deny the Problem

Joseph knew his brothers had rejected him and had nothing but hateful, evil intentions for him. He didn't deny that they hurt him deeply. When he saw them years later, he didn't throw open his arms and accept them as if nothing had ever happened. You may be a victim of rejection or abuse. Don't deny the problem! Don't deny the hurt!

If someone punches you in the eye and then later pleads for forgiveness with a sorrowful confession and heartfelt repentance, what do you think that's going to do for your eye? Suppose you show up at church two weeks later and a friend notices that you still have a black eye. Your friend might say, "Didn't you forgive him? If you would forgive, your hurt would be gone! You know what they say, 'Forgive and forget.'" Pretty silly, wouldn't you say? It's the same with our emotions. Whether repentance and forgiveness are applied to the wound or not, *healing still takes time*!

He Kept God's Agenda

Joseph knew that God had a plan for him, and he wasn't about to let anything destroy it, including his brothers. He knew his brothers' deceitful hearts, so he kept a cautious distance and tested their motives and the truth of their words (see Genesis 42). Just as God was with Joseph through his abuse and imprisonment, He will be with you and will turn what was intended for evil into good. However, *this does not mean you should abandon caution and open the door for more abuse.*

You cannot expect anyone else to value you if you don't value yourself. God values you so much that He sent His Son to die for you. You are valuable! But God doesn't want you to let someone else destroy your body (His temple) with emotional or physical abuse.

He Ministered Reconciliation

Reconciliation means "to make things right or to restore a relationship." After protecting himself and God's purpose in his life from any additional harm, Joseph's final step was to minister reconciliation. He reached out with a pure heart of forgiveness, because he saw that God's love and His purposes were bigger than his pain and their plan to hurt him. Remember, nothing can cancel out the call of God on your life but your allowing someone or something to paralyze you from your purpose.

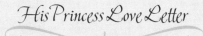

His Princess Love Letter

My Princess,

I am here with you desiring to be the shoulder your tears fall on. When you hurt I hurt, and it breaks My heart to watch you cry without Me. I too walked the world broken, My love. We will work through any and all things together, My Bride. I can and will heal your broken heart. Call out My name, Jesus, in your dark hours and I will hold you. Will you give Me a chance to love you back to life again? I promise that you will see the light of a new day, and joy will come again and you will smile!

Love,
Your Prince
who will wipe away your tears

His Princess in Action

Read the story of Joseph in chapters 37–47 of Genesis.

If you or someone you know is in a toxic love relationship, get help. Call a good Christian church that has a ministry support group for these types of unhealthy, toxic relationships.

He will once again fill your mouth with laughter
and your lips with shouts of joy.

Job 8:21 NLT[2]

Treasure of Truth for Today

If you are constantly being victimized by the symptoms of toxic love, you are no longer a victim—you are a volunteer!

Looking for His Attention

May you experience the love of Christ, though it is so great you will never fully understand it. Then you will be filled with the fullness of life and power that comes from God.

Ephesians 3:19 NLT[1]

I had grown up in California where slim, toned, and tan people strut around confidently in bathing suits all the time, and where I never appeared in public without a cover-up or some other form of camouflage that would hide my overweight, not-so-perfect body. So when I finally lost sixty pounds during my senior year, I was elated about being thin and able to show off my new body in a swimsuit. (Keep in mind, this was before I became a Christian.)

It was time for my coming-out party.

A national volleyball tournament was going to be held on the beach, and I was determined to make a good impression. . . . In a big way, I was going to make up for all those fat jokes and lost time! I knew there would be national media coverage of the tournament and that sports agents and casting directors would be looking for new talent. I was determined to get the attention I'd always longed for.

I arrived at the beach tournament in a white swimsuit, with a white towel, white sunglasses, white hat, with little white sandals to match, a white fold-out chair, big rhinestone earrings, my makeup on perfectly, and my hair freshly styled. I made a royal entrance, flashing my best beauty pageant smile and parting the sea of wide-eyed weekend wayfarers with my radiantly white ensemble. Despite the urge, I refrained from doing my little pageant wave.

Everybody was looking at me. I didn't care that I was the only person on the beach who looked like she had been getting dressed to attend a formal dinner and then suddenly decided to go watch a volleyball game instead.

I imagined casting directors rushing to see who could get to me first. They were no doubt assuring each other, "She's obviously the next Hollywood megastar."

Thousands of people had gathered for the tournament. Thousands of people means lots of food. In California lots of food means lots of seagulls—flocks and swarms of seagulls. And we all know what lots of seagulls eating lots of food eventually generate.

My elegant and perfectly positioned hat was too tempting a target to pass up. Of all the people they could have chosen to unload upon, the seagull bombardiers chose the one in dazzling white who was busily making a lasting impression. Little did their target know how lasting her impression was soon to become.

My ensemble had attracted plenty of admiring onlookers, but no one was watching the sky as an enemy seagull opened the bomb bay doors high overhead. In other words, all eyes were on me when a big (and I mean humongous) blob of seagull poop landed—*splurff*—on the edge of my hat. With an impeccable sense of timing, it lingered briefly on the brim before proceeding to drip into my perfectly styled hair.

Summoning what shred of poise I could, I removed my hat (carefully), cleaned up my hair and hat with my towel, and wished I could sink beneath the sand without a trace. My regal aura was shattered. I definitely got the attention of an adoring audience. All eyes were on me, all mouths were laughing, and all fingers were pointing. What a mess I was a part of! Literally.

The Word of God says, "Humble yourselves before the Lord, and he will lift you up" (James 4:10). At that time in my life I was too busy lifting up Sheri Rose to pay any attention to God. My big day at the beach was an unforgettable lesson in humility. When we try to exalt ourselves above others, we set ourselves up to be dumped on. To make this point clear, God will use whatever it takes—dive-bombing seagulls included—to get our eyes on Him and off ourselves.

His Princess Prayer

Dear Lord,

Let Your love and attention be enough for me. Forgive me for the times I seek man's approval more than Yours. May knowing that You love and adore me be all I ever need and crave.

In Your name I pray, Amen

His Princess in Action

Take a moment and write down the right reasons to become your best. Then say a short prayer and ask the Lord to search your heart to see if His attention is enough for you.

Treasure of Truth for Today

His love and attention fills more than our hearts;
it satisfies our souls.

Day 16

"I'll Be Happy When . . ."

There is a way that seems right to a man,
but in the end it leads to death.

Proverbs 14:12

efore I became a Christian, my life was a book with a sleek and colorful cover, but inside the pages were empty. Each chapter of what looked like my new life had the same title, "I'll Be Happy When . . ."

I followed my own personal success strategies, learned by carefully examining the latest research from all the top celebrities on television and in the magazines:

- *Strategy 1*: I had no basis for right and wrong . . . I just followed my feelings.
- *Strategy 2*: I bought things I didn't need to impress people I didn't really care about with money I didn't have.
- *Strategy 3*: I made excuses and blamed others because it was easier than accepting responsibility for my own actions.
- *Strategy 4*: I refused to forgive those who had hurt me, and I held on to bitterness and resentment.
- *Strategy 5*: My problems, my happiness, my success, and my entertainment consumed me.

- *Strategy 6*: I was anxious for everything and let all my requests be made known to anyone who would listen.

My personal success strategies left me emotionally starving, lonely, and depressed because money, things, worldly success, and beauty could only hide my pain; they could not heal it. Our ways will never get us what we really want.

God's plan is the key to being set free from depression, food addictions, eating disorders, and emotional pain.

He whom the Son has set free is free indeed!

His Princess Prayer

My Lord,

How many times I struggle to believe You are truly here with me. Even though You have proved Your presence over and over again, I still allow my heart to doubt. So here I am again, requesting that You will become more real to me than ever before. Please come comfort me once again that I may find my faith in You again. Thank You for Your never-ending patience with Your Princess.

In Jesus' name I pray, Amen

His Princess in Action

Read the Scripture below and seek Him now in prayer.

"You will seek me and find me when you seek me with all your heart. I will be found by you," declares the LORD, "and will bring you back from captivity."

Jeremiah 29:13–14

Treasure of Truth for Today

He is our strength when we're weak.
He is our comfort when we're in pain.
He is our peace when we're haunted by fear.
He is our healer when our spirit is wounded.
He is our warmth when the world is cold.
He is our power when we need a miracle.

Anger Happens!

*Understand this, my dear brothers and sisters: You must all be
quick to listen, slow to speak, and slow to get angry.*

James 1:19 NLT[2]

ave you ever been told that you shouldn't feel angry,
that being angry is ungodly? Did you know there are
benefits to anger?

Anger is an emotion—designed by God—to reveal that your
spirit has been attacked, provoked, or wounded. What we do
with anger depends on whether we are being led by God's Spirit
or by our flesh. If we are controlled by our flesh, then anger will
trigger a sinful attitude or action. If we respond this way, we will
fall into a dangerous rut that may cause extreme damage to others and ourselves physically, emotionally, and spiritually.

If, on the other hand, our spirit is led by God's Spirit, anger
will still trigger a response, but this time God will be honored.
Ephesians 4:26 says, "Be angry, and yet do not sin; do not let the
sun go down on your anger" (NASB). Anger is not a sin, but we
must do something with it before the sun goes down.

A prominent Christian leader told of a conference where he
was speaking. In the front row of every session he taught, there
sat a woman and her husband. The man struggled to stay awake
during the conference, but by the middle of the day he was sleep-

ing soundly—even snoring. Needless to say, the Christian speaker was perturbed by this rude behavior, and he struggled with anger throughout the conference. Immediately after the last session, Rip Van Winkle and his wife hastily approached the speaker.

"Oh, we are so thrilled to finally meet you!" the wife gushed. "We enjoyed your speaking so much. We can't believe how blessed we are to be here! You see, my husband has a rare medical disorder, and his doctors have only given him a few more weeks to live. His last request was to fly wherever you are just to hear you speak."

The well-known Christian leader was humbled and embarrassed by his attitude. His anger had revealed a lack of understanding.

Remember, it is okay to feel angry. Whether that anger triggers a sinful attitude or action is up to us.

His Princess Prayer

Dear Lord,

I confess I do not always handle my anger well. Please grab hold of my heart and help me to respond in a way that will bring glory to Your name. I want and need to be led through this trial by Your Spirit, not my feelings. Give me wisdom and show me the areas I need to get right with You and others.

In Jesus' name I pray, Amen

His Princess in Action

1. *Stop! Wait!* Make a conscious effort to acknowledge who's in control—your flesh or God's Spirit.

2. *Think the situation through.* To what are you reacting? Is your spirit being attacked or provoked? Or is your flesh being exposed? Remember, our flesh refuses to die willingly. It will jump to defend itself at every opportunity.

3. *Look at the offender's heart.* Is there something you don't fully understand about this situation? Look at your own heart to make sure you are being controlled by God's Spirit.

4. *Admit your feelings to God.* Don't repress your anger. Ask God to give you understanding. Look for what God is trying to reveal about your own spirit—or your flesh.

5. *Decide on the most appropriate action.* Jesus had complete understanding and acted righteously when His anger triggered an aggressive response, causing Him to clear the money changers and wicked merchants out of the temple court. Perhaps you have lost a child in a drunk-driving accident; as a result, your anger may have motivated you to gain understanding and to get involved with Mothers Against Drunk Drivers.

Treasure of Truth for Today

He who is slow to anger has great understanding,
But he who is quick-tempered exalts folly.

Proverbs 14:29 NASB

A Spirit-to-Spirit Relationship

May the grace of the Lord Jesus Christ, the love of God, and the
fellowship of the Holy Spirit be with you all.

2 Corinthians 13:14 NLT[2]

od wants to have a Spirit-to-spirit relationship with you—not just an intellectual one, although many have settled for that. Many are "acquainted" with God by hearing others talk about Him or perhaps by occasionally reading the Bible. They simply don't understand that God wants to give them so much more.

In fact, some of the most brilliant men and women in all the world have missed out on discovering their human spirit and the opportunity to have Spirit-to-spirit relationships with the Creator of the universe! Even Nicodemus, one of the most intellectually gifted religious leaders of his day, could not grasp it. When Jesus told him he must be born again in order to enter the kingdom of God, Nicodemus shook his head in confusion—he was thinking and reasoning only in physical terms. Jesus responded by saying, "That which is born of the flesh is flesh; and that which is born of the Spirit is spirit" (John 3:6 KJV).

So what does this relationship with God look like?

If you and I wanted to know more about Tom Cruise, we could go to Beverly Hills and take a guided tour that stops in front of his house. We could even read all about his life in newspaper and magazine articles. But imagine if we were touring Tom's house and he actually opened the door and invited you in to visit with Katie and their child. That would be entirely different. You would be forming a relationship with the Cruise family. (Now, back to reality!) Have you ever toured the house of God? Probably. Ever read about Him? Heard those awesome Red Sea stories? Maybe. But do you understand that God Himself has invited you inside? That He loves you and wants to have a relationship with you?

My dad had a satellite dish at his home in San Diego. It was ten feet across and could pick up every video broadcast known to man. Every May, he would call me on the phone just before I would sit down to watch the national telecast of the Miss USA Beauty Pageant. Without fail, he would predict which contestants would be selected for the top ten. Halfway through the telecast he would call me back and tell me that he had a "gut feeling" that Miss "So-and-So" was going to win. He drove me crazy, until I figured out that his satellite dish was picking up the video signals an hour before I was! (He was such a sneak!) Now, when I sit down to watch a nationally televised pageant, I know not to answer the phone.

Just like my dad's satellite receiver, we each have a satellite dish of sorts within us. God has wired us to be "tuned in" to basically two channels—the physical and the spiritual. The physical channel operates through our brain, and we respond mechanically or intellectually; the spiritual channel operates through our heart, and we respond emotionally. Unfortunately, it is more natural for us to respond to life by developing and nourishing only our mental and intellectual capabilities. So, likewise, it's natural to believe that our success in work, school, social life, and relationships depends entirely on our intellect, and when we can't make mental sense of it all, we grow frustrated, depressed, lonely, and unfulfilled.

God loves you and wants to live inside you and through you. When you open your spirit to Him, you'll discover that He longs to touch your every hurt, heal your deepest pain, revive your fainting heart, and soar with you over every mountain.

His Princess Prayer

Dear Jesus,

I want to connect with You. How I long to feel You close to me. I want to walk through this life knowing the Savior of the world is thinking of me. May I never stop looking for You as You continue to reveal Your love to me each new day. Let me never forget I am Yours. I am ready to be closer to You than ever before.

In Your name I pray, Amen

His Princess in Action

Open your Bible right now and ask the Lord to speak to your spirit through His Word. You will find a word just for you from your Father in heaven.

Treasure of Truth for Today

When you can't feel Him walking with you,
He is carrying you.

Royal Preparation

If you try to hang on to your life, you will lose it. But if you give up your life for my sake, you will save it.

Matthew 16:25 NLT[2]

he royal preparation is designed to strengthen your character so you will be ready to handle the attacks of the enemy—an enemy who wants to destroy God's kingdom. Every mighty man or woman of God has gone through this preparation. Without it, they would not have been equipped to live out their royal call!

The call is not about *comfort*; it's about *character*. David was in a cave during his preparation for his royal call. Joseph was in a prison during his preparation to become chief adviser to Pharoah. Queen Esther's preparation gave her the courage to risk her life to save her people. The purpose of this call is not about pain; it's about power. It's not about trials; it's about triumph. Great battles bring great victory.

Several years ago, God moved my heart to help those with hidden pain. Sometimes I would feel their pain so deeply that I would weep uncontrollably. Because of the royal preparation God allowed me to go through, I knew in my spirit that there were millions who carried pain no one could see on the outside. I wanted to use my healing and new life in Christ to help women around the world unveil their pain so they could have victory in their life.

Through praying, God revealed to me His Princess Ministries. I was as excited as a pregnant woman who can't wait to see her baby! As I began to take the necessary steps for this ministry, I had no idea how hard the labor pains would be before the ministry was actually birthed.

Today, I can honestly say that this royal call has been worth every trial, every pain, and every tear I've had to cry to see the more than half-million women I have ministered to at women's retreats.

I've learned that for us to live out our royal call, we will have to walk away from some of the comforts and pleasures in this world.

The most important thing when entering into your calling is "to be faithful with little and He will give you much." All of us are in preparation for a royal call. In fact, God has an incredible call on your life.

The question is, Will you answer it?

His Princess Prayer

Dear Lord,

I want to answer the royal call You have on my life. Use my pain for Your greater purpose. Take the tears I have cried and make me tender toward others. Take my passion and make me passionate for You. I want You to open whatever gift You have

*placed inside my soul and prepare me for great
things that will bring glory to You.*
  In Jesus' name I pray, Amen

His Princess in Action

Write down what you do well or love to do . . .

Where are you the most effective? Think for a moment about
something you love to do, something that energizes you and gives
you joy and that you do well (e.g., organizing, directing, serving,
writing, teaching, singing, working with children, decorating,
counseling, coordinating, hosting, cooking, volunteering).

Treasure of Truth for Today

What you are willing to walk away from
will determine how much God can bring to you.

Day 20

A Deep, Dark Secret

Finally, I confessed all my sins to you
  and stopped trying to hide my guilt.
I said to myself, "I will confess my rebellion to the LORD."
  And you forgave me! All my guilt is gone.

Psalm 32:5 NLT[2]

thought I was totally free from the shame of my past until one day after I became pregnant with our first child. On that afternoon the shame surfaced again . . .

My husband and I were so excited about going to the doctor to confirm that, yes, we were going to have a baby. There I was, lying on the doctor's table, when he asked me if I wanted to hear my baby's heartbeat. I said, "How is that possible? I'm only six weeks pregnant." Long ago I had been told—wrongly—that babies don't have heartbeats until they are at least twenty weeks old.

The doctor put the stethoscope to my tummy, and for the very first time I heard the beat of my son's heart. I began to cry.

My husband thought I was crying tears of joy. However, the truth is that I was crying tears of pain and regret—even terror! How could such a miraculous moment bring that reaction?

Distant memories flooded my mind. I choked back my tears as I recalled an afternoon twelve years earlier. I was only sixteen at the time, but lying on that doctor's table suddenly made it feel as if it were yesterday. One unwise mistake with a guy, and I had found myself pregnant. An abortion, the doctor told me, was the right thing to do: "It's only been six weeks. It's not a baby. It doesn't even have a heartbeat," he assured me.

Now I was confronted for the first time with the horrifying truth about that long-ago decision—and I was too ashamed to tell my husband. For several more years I lived with such shame and fear that I was sure God would take my son in order to punish me. I didn't know how there was any way I could get right with God for something so wrong—something that had happened so long ago.

My Prince finally rescued me over Easter weekend in 1999. It was Good Friday night, and we were at church. A big wooden cross had been displayed in the sanctuary. Each of us was holding a big nail and a small piece of paper. Then the pastor told the story of Easter unlike I had ever heard it before. When he finished, he invited anyone who was holding on to past sin or shame to write it on the paper, walk forward, pick up a hammer, and nail it to the cross. I thought, *Can my Lord really remove the guilty stains and wipe away my shame?* I sat there paralyzed by my fear of what people would think if I walked forward.

Finally, I felt the Spirit of God whisper, "Give Me your past. Give Me your shame." I got up and walked toward the cross. The moment I picked up that hammer and drove the nail through my confessed sin, I felt the Lord whisper in my spirit, "This is why I had to die for you—so I could take away all your guilt and shame."

At that moment He replaced my past pain with His peace.

His Princess Love Letter

My pure Princess,

I have covered you with My blood. I loved you with My life. I don't see you the way you see yourself. That is why I paid the ultimate price for any and all things that you have ever done. You are My spotless and pure Bride. Should you refuse to receive My forgiveness, My love, you are saying My death on the cross was not enough for you. When you ask forgiveness, I cast your sin in the sea of forgetfulness and remember it no more. Now is the time for you to celebrate your new life in Me!

Love,
Your Savior and Purity

His Princess in Action

If you are holding on to something, maybe it's time for you to look at the cross as more than a symbol of your Savior's death. When our Lord died and rose again, He broke forever the power of sin on our lives. Right now, take a moment and invite the Lord to search your heart for any unresolved sin from your past that continues to torment you.

> *But he was pierced for our transgressions,*
> *he was crushed for our iniquities;*
> *the punishment that brought us peace was upon him,*
> *and by his wounds we are healed.*
>
> *Isaiah 53:5*

Treasure of Truth for Today

When we refuse to forgive ourselves, we are saying by our actions that the cross was not enough.

Day 21

The Disease of Loneliness

Two people are better off than one, for they can help each other succeed. If one person falls, the other can reach out and help. But someone who falls alone is in real trouble.

Ecclesiastes 4:9–10 NLT[2]

Mother Teresa was once asked, "How can we restore peace to our world?" Her answer was simply this: "Go home and learn to love one another." When she was asked what the worst disease facing humankind was, this tiny woman, who had spent her life in sacrificial service ministering in Calcutta to the sick and the dying, answered that the greatest disease was loneliness, especially in America.

Maybe our comforts and conveniences are getting in the way of the very thing we need most . . . one another. Loneliness, like cancer, may not manifest any symptoms at first. We suffer on the inside but appear to be fine on the outside. We smile to people at work, we sing in the pew at church, and we do a good job keeping our "life is great and I'm happy" look on our faces. Yet, if we were really honest with ourselves, many of us would say, "I feel so alone."

Why do we suffer in quiet, lonely desperation? Maybe we don't want to appear weak or needy. Instead, we choose to stay isolated. We create an image that says, "I am secure on my own." The enemy of our soul loves it when we do this. In fact, he tries to separate us from other people. That is one of his most important and often unrecognized strategies. When a lion is hungry, the king of beasts doesn't go after the whole herd. He can't defeat a herd, and he doesn't even try. Instead, he goes after an isolated animal. Likewise, the devil tries to separate an unsuspecting victim from the body of believers. His goal is to isolate the weak because he sees past the painted smile on our face. We might as well paint a bull's-eye on our chest and say, "Come and get me, Satan! I'm alone."

His Princess Prayer

Dear God,

I do feel lonely. Many times I am too afraid to reach out to someone. I fear I may be rejected or get hurt. Please give me the courage to conquer this lonely place I am in. Help me to love others as You love me, unconditionally.

In Jesus' name, Amen

His Princess in Action

The best cure for loneliness is to serve one another in some sort of ministry. Go out today and sign up for a small group

Bible study, or sign up to volunteer once a week through a charity or ministry at your church. There are so many options: children's ministry, choir, outreach, greeter, and women's ministry.

Treasure of Truth for Today

Those who refresh others will themselves be refreshed.

Proverbs 11:25 NLT[2]

Day 22

Forgive Yourself

Oh, what joy for those
whose disobedience is forgiven,
whose sin is put out of sight!
Yes, what joy for those
whose record the Lord has cleared of guilt,
whose lives are lived in complete honesty!

Psalm 32:1–2 NLT[2]

This step toward freedom somehow seems the hardest. For some reason, we feel we don't know how to forgive ourselves for what's gone wrong. But without forgiving yourself, you can't become emotionally free, and you will remain frozen by your failures.

You can never change anything you have said or done in your past, but you can learn from it and let it go!

Who could have a better reason for not forgiving himself than the apostle Peter? He had walked with Jesus, and his life had been changed forever by this friend. Yet when tough times hit, he denied that he had ever even known his friend—not once, but three times! Imagine if Peter had never forgiven himself for denying Jesus. If he had allowed his failures to paralyze him, he would never have finished God's call on his life—the call to be the "rock" upon which Christ would later build His church! (See Matthew 16:18.)

We are called to leave a legacy as Peter was. The old has passed and the new has come. Yesterday is in the past, tomorrow is in the future, but today is a gift and that is why it is called "the present." However, if we wake up every morning feeling guilty, we will not be able to receive the gifts our God wants to give us or become a gift to others.

Forgive yourself today. Don't allow the enemy of your emotions to remind you of your sin. God has taken the load of sin and guilt off your back and has thrown it into the "sea of forgetfulness." You have no business hanging around the seashore with a fishing pole and a net trying to retrieve it. Leave it there and move on with God!

His Princess Prayer

Dear Lord,

You have given Your life for my mistakes, and all You require in return is that I receive Your gift of a new day and a new life. It is so hard to believe that all I have ever done wrong is lost in Your sea of forgetfulness. May I walk the rest of my days as Your forgiven Princess.

In Jesus' name I pray, Amen

His Princess in Action

Write a letter to your Lord, thanking Him that you are truly forgiven.

Treasure of Truth for Today

Princesses are not perfect . . . the pressure is off.

A Divinely Designed Day

But you are not like that, for you are a chosen people. You are royal priests, a holy nation, God's very own possession. As a result, you can show others the goodness of God, for he called you out of the darkness into his wonderful light.

1 Peter 2:9 NLT²

 had just finished speaking in New York City on the royal call in 1 Peter 2:9. "If we pray for a divine appointment to share the gospel every day," I said confidently, "God will give us one."

The pastor of the church where I spoke, along with his wife, spent the next day sightseeing with my husband Steve and me. Before we started out, the pastor suggested, "Let's pray for one of those divine appointments you've been talking about."

What a great idea, I thought. This is the Big Apple. There certainly couldn't be a shortage of hurting people here.

We prayed and then set out to make the rounds of all the famous tourist attractions. We saw the Statue of Liberty, drank tea at the Plaza Hotel, ice-skated at Rockefeller Center, and saw the World Trade Center. But as the sun set over the Jersey shore, not a single door had been opened for a divine appointment.

I was getting ready to trip someone so I could pick them up, apologize, and tell them about Jesus.

About 10:00 p.m. it happened: we stopped in a coffee shop for a bite to eat before heading back to our hotel for the night. Two young girls came up to me, and one of them asked, "Are you a celebrity?"

Recognizing my cue, I said, "Yes. I am a daughter of the King. My Father created the heavens and the earth."

Finally my appointment had showed up. The two girls looked at each other, then back at me. "What does that mean?" the other one asked.

"Well, Jesus is my Savior," I explained. "So that means I have a relationship with God, and that makes me His daughter. My God is the King of kings and Lord of lords."

We talked with the two girls all the way through their dinner. After half an hour, one of the girls said, "I could never accept this Jesus and become a daughter of the King because I'm Jewish."

"What a coincidence!" I exclaimed. "So am I! And so is my Savior." I shared my testimony with the girls, and Steve shared Scriptures with them about God's eternal plan for their lives. As I was going over all that God had done in my life—how He had delivered me out of drug abuse, bulimia, a broken heart, and a broken home—one of the girls started to cry. "I just got out of a drug rehab program last week," she said. "Say, are you guys angels?"

"No," I answered, "but we are messengers, and this is the divine appointment we prayed for this morning. You see, God arranged for us to meet you here today so that we could give you a message of hope and eternal life. And now we would love to invite you to become daughters of the King yourselves and receive the eternal crown, so that you can experience God's peace in your life today and enjoy His presence for all eternity."

Right there in the restaurant, those two girls accepted Jesus as their Savior and became daughters of the King. What a wonderful, glorious day it was! How different the story would have been if all Steve and I had had to talk about was how rude New Yorkers are, how expensive the food is, and how much our feet hurt. Every day, our steps are ordered of the Lord, and our conversation can cause people to thirst for righteousness in Christ.

His Princess Prayer

Dear Lord,

I ask You on this day to order my steps. Don't let me miss what You have for me to do today. Please forgive me for all the days I was so consumed with me that I forgot about Your plan. I am ready and willing to walk with You today and be Your light to this dark world.

In Jesus' name, Amen

His Princess in Action

Go to your King today and pray for Him to set up a divine appointment for you. Your day will go from ordinary to extraordinary.

Treasure of Truth for Today

A day designed by the King is royally refreshing!

The Pretender

Then you will know the truth, and the truth will set you free.

John 8:32

Many have asked me how I finally broke free from food and past pain controlling my life. My answer is, I always cry out to my Father in heaven when I hurt. I have learned the hard way that I am not strong enough to handle life alone.

The truth is, when we take our mask off, we not only free ourselves to become all God created us to be, we help others to become real. Our God is very real with us, and nothing is more comforting than knowing we can be ourselves with the Lord and with those we love.

When a warning light comes on in a car, putting a piece of black tape over the warning light won't fix the car. It needs to be taken to a mechanic, one who knows how the car works and understands how to fix it. Some people drive through life ignoring all the warning lights until one day they find themselves broken down in a ditch somewhere. Don't wait—fix it now!

I didn't deal with my pain. I covered up my warning signs. My life did break down, and I was forced to face my feelings the night I almost lost my life to a drug overdose. The emotional roller coaster I lived on warned me of danger, but I didn't know what to do or where to turn. It wasn't long before I derailed and crashed. Suddenly, I was thrown onto a road of reality. I had to face the fact that I was a drug-addicted, D-student, self-destructive teenager going nowhere in life. I had to "get real" with who I was and who I was becoming. A few years later, I did finally fall to my knees in severe emotional pain and cried out to the Lord, and He comforted me.

Somehow we women have bought the lie that being spiritual requires denying how we really feel. Our Daddy in heaven cares more about how we feel than anyone, and He is the only one who can remove the stone we placed over our hearts to protect ourselves and who can set us free!

His Princess Prayer

Dear Abba Father,

Wipe away my tears once again. Lord, help me to trust You and cry out to You. Even though I cannot see You, I am taking a step of faith and giving You all my fears, tears, and disappointments. Release me and help me cry out to You so I can be free as You love me back to life again.

I pray in Jesus' name, Amen

His Princess in Action

Do you ever tell Him about your anger, bitterness, jealousy, resentment, or hatred? Sounds ungodly, doesn't it? Have you ever thought to yourself, *I shouldn't be feeling this way? Why can't I be joyful about this?*

It's time to get real with God. Voice to God your bitterness, your jealousy, your envy, your hatred, and your resentment. If we are not honest about our emotions, covering up the warning signals of our spirit, we will slowly die inwardly. God is a God of truth.

> *He will once again fill your mouth with laughter*
> *and your lips with shouts of joy.*
>
> *Job 8:21 NLT*[2]

Treasure of Truth for Today

Tears to the Lord are the hidden treasure to
refresh our soul and renew our strength.

Fight the Good Fight!

I have fought a good fight, I have finished the race, and I have remained faithful. And now the prize awaits me—the crown of righteousness that the Lord, the righteous Judge, will give me on that great day of his return. And the prize is not just for me but for all who eagerly look forward to his glorious return!

2 Timothy 4:7–8 NLT[1]

Too many times when problems arise we turn to food to get us through the storm. How many times have we said, "I will diet when I get through this trial"? Or "When life is less stressful, then I will take care of myself"? Think about this next time you are craving a perfect life:

King Solomon had it all—wealth, women, power, servants. Yet, in the book of Ecclesiastes the wisest king who ever lived describes life as meaningless. How could that be?

There was only one thing that King Solomon did not have: a battle to fight. However, his father King David fought many battles in his lifetime. He fought a battle against a giant in the land who was coming against God's people. His courage and faith birthed his public ministry and made him a spiritual hero. David fought battles against countless enemies, which carved character and prepared him for the royal call God had on his life. He battled with insecurity, so he waited in a cave for his calling, and that battle helped him find his confidence in

God alone. He was also in a battle for his very life while Saul was trying to have him killed. His battle with fear for his life birthed real faith within the future king. And in his pain he wrote many of the psalms we read today in the Bible. He had a battle with his father, who did not even consider David as the son who could have been chosen by God to become the future king.

The interesting thing to me is that the one time David was not fighting a battle, he fell into sin with Bathsheba and had her husband killed to cover his sin.

Many times our battles in this life prepare us for our purpose. So the goal in our walk with God should not be to dodge the pain and problems this life brings, but to learn to fight the good fight and finish strong! Wouldn't it be great to be able to say at the end of our days on this earth as Paul did in 2 Timothy 4:7, "I have fought the good fight"?

We won't have the strength to fight the good fight if we don't eat right, exercise, and rest. Our bodies are like a tricycle. The big wheel in the front is the Spirit who lives within us. The right wheel in the back is our emotions, which need to be controlled by the front wheel, the Spirit. The left wheel is our physical bodies in which the Holy Spirit reigns inside. Our strength to fight is based on how well we learn to balance all three of these wheels that carry us through life.

We all feel out of balance sometimes. Don't ignore the warning signs of being tipped too far one way or the other. Stop and ask the Lord to show you what wheel needs attention. It is so worth taking the time to fix the bike before we tip over and fall. A well-balanced life is a blessing to ourselves and others.

His Princess Prayer

Dear Lord,

Too many times I have run to the refrigerator for refuge instead of to You. Help me stop. I want to allow You to feed me when I feel overwhelmed by life. I want the peace You promise as I walk through this life. I ask Your forgiveness for the excuses I have made to trash Your temple by eating foods that make me sick and tired. May I never miss another day to live for You!

In Jesus' name I pray, Amen

His Princess in Action

In Matthew 11:28 Jesus said, "Come to me, all of you who are weary and carry heavy burdens, and I will give you rest" (NLT[2]). Right now give Him those burdens you carry by writing them in a letter and putting the letter in your Bible.

Treasure of Truth for Today

Trade a piece of cake or chocolate for "His peace."

Day 26

What Kind of Princess Are You?

We have different gifts, according to the grace given us. If a man's gift is prophesying, let him use it in proportion to his faith. If it is serving, let him serve; if it is teaching, let him teach; if it is encouraging, let him encourage; if it is contributing to the needs of others, let him give generously; if it is leadership, let him govern diligently; if it is showing mercy, let him do it cheerfully.

Romans 12:6–8

We have been divinely designed and appointed for a position in our lives. A lot of times our overeating and food addictions are just a side effect of not understanding the way we are wired by God Himself. Read below and see if you can find yourself:

PRINCESS SERVER

If you have the gift of service, you naturally see needs the rest of us don't see. You know how to take care of others, and you find and spread joy in helping make caring things happen.

You are an excellent example of how Jesus wants us to serve one another.

Princess Teacher

If you have the gift of teaching, you are the watchdog of the Christian army. You can discern truth, you can teach us, and you can help us better understand the King's truth.

We could not survive the battle without you. We could not obey our King's commands if you did not teach us how to get right with God. You are an excellent example of how to live with deep conviction in our hearts.

Princess Encourager

If you have the gift of encouragement, you are our spiritual cheerleader. We need you especially when someone or something has wounded us. You help us keep fighting the good fight. You remind us of the King's eternal truths, and you help us soar to new heights in life in Him. You are an excellent example of how to build each other up in our faith.

Princess Giver

If you have the gift of giving, you help supply our spiritual and practical needs. You also teach us to be generous, and you help us discover the true joy of giving.

Your gift goes beyond giving to far-reaching and life-changing charitable organizations, and you have a great desire to see God's kingdom advance. You are an excellent example of what it means to invest in eternity.

PRINCESS LEADER

If you have the gift of leadership, you get things done; you make things happen. Without you, we would not have retreats, conventions, or order in the church. You see the big picture, you know how to direct people where they can best serve, and you help dreams become reality. You are an excellent example of what it means to put our purpose into action.

PRINCESS MERCY

If you have the gift of mercy, you are part of the nervous system of the body of Christ. You feel our pain, you share our burdens, you listen to us with your whole heart, and you show us how to serve others deeply. When you share your gift, you show us God's mercy, and you help us get through life's tough times. You are an excellent example of how to show God's tenderness to the world.

PRINCESS PROPHET

If you have the gift of prophecy, then you are naturally strong in your convictions. You can give us courage to stand for righteousness and lead us to victory as you boldly stand up against the enemy of our souls by exposing sin. You are an excellent example of what it means to fear God more than man.

His Princess Prayer

Dear Lord,

I am ready to settle into who You created me to be. Help me to use the strengths You have given me to be a blessing. Forgive me for judging others for not responding to life the way I do. Help all of Your daughters complete one another, and forgive us for competing with each other.

In Jesus' name I pray, Amen

His Princess in Action

Take a moment to write down your passion and some long-lost dream, then set a goal and move toward what it is you're called to do.

Treasure of Truth for Today

Use your gift to bless others rather than impress others, and it will be received with deep appreciation.

What Is Eating You Inside?

Do not take revenge, my friends, but leave room for God's wrath, for it is written: "It is mine to avenge; I will repay," says the Lord.

Romans 12:19

What makes our hearts melt when we sit in the theater and watch a great love story? It's not the hero's physical strength or his beloved's beauty. You and I are drawn to the power of true love and its inexplicable ability to prevail despite tragedy and hardship. (Often the greater the conflict, the greater the love.)

We run into problems, though, when we get accustomed to seeing relational problems solved in the time it takes to eat a bag of popcorn and drink a soda. Our hero and his beauty have less than two hours to defeat the dragons and overcome unspeakable challenges (even less time if we're watching a situation comedy on TV, where relational conflicts magically resolve themselves in less than thirty minutes)! You and I are not going to magically resolve any relationship in our own wisdom, and definitely not in less than two hours. However, the Author of love, our Prince of Peace, has written a script. His Word on real-life royal relationships can lead us to the happy ending we long for!

Many of us have been wounded by someone, and it is hard to let go of that pain. Let's take a moment and look at King David's example of handling a fierce King Saul, who once loved David but grew bitterly jealous and envious of the call God had on the future king's life. David was running from a man who was trying to hurt, hinder, and even kill him. Yet David, in God's strength, was able to resist the temptation to kill his enemy when he came upon the sleeping King Saul. From a human perspective David had good reason to kill Saul. He had made David's life miserable and was now seeking to kill him; Saul was after David without a just reason. Even Saul's son Jonathan took David's side during the hunt. But David, the future anointed king, did something much greater than take revenge: he deferred to God's will and obeyed the command not to strike down the man God had placed on the throne. In other words, he did what his God wanted him to do.

Many of us will never experience the magnitude of God's great call on our lives until we give revenge, regret, and our rights back to the Lord.

His Princess Prayer

Dear Lord,

I give You _____ (person's name), and I trust You to deal with this person who has hurt me so badly. I do not want to carry this pain any longer. You are a just God, and I choose to trust You. Starting today I release this bitterness that has burrowed its way into my soul. Please heal my

heart once again and teach me what You want me
to learn in this circumstance.
In Jesus' name I pray, Amen

His Princess in Action

Is there a King Saul in your life—someone you need to leave to God's care even though you have real reasons to act in revenge? Follow King David's example and let God deal with those who have caused you pain and suffering. If you will do what God wants you to do, you will find the freedom that comes along with doing what is right in God's sight. He will deal with those who have hurt His daughters! Write a letter to your Lord and give that person to Him right now.

Treasure of Truth for Today

Care more about God's will than your rights,
and you will win victory.

Day 28

Get Ready for Your Prince to Come

The wedding day of the Lamb is here, and his bride is ready. She will be given a wedding dress made of pure and shining linen. This linen stands for the good things God's people have done.

Revelation 19:7 NLT[2]

The bride-to-be stood motionless, staring in the mirror for what seemed like an eternity. She had worked hard preparing for this moment. Her hair and makeup were a work of art, and her dress was stunning. Never before had she felt so beautiful. But something was missing. Where were her guests? Had she not made it clear to everyone that this day was coming? The greatest day the world would ever know? An open guest book sat beside her—blank. The gift table—empty . . . except for a stack of unopened letters.

The bride sifted through the pile looking for something without really knowing what. Tears of joy filled her eyes as she read the familiar phrase her Prince had written on the envelope:

I can't wait to see you face-to-face, My dearest Princess! I love you!

A sense of eagerness overcame her, and she began to open the envelope. But just then, she heard the sound of the most beautiful music in the distance, more beautiful than she had ever heard before. It was time . . . the wedding march had begun!

She dropped the letter and ran toward the large double doors that opened into the gloriously decorated sanctuary. The anointed sweet music filled the empty hall. She wrestled with these unanswered questions as she slowly walked down the aisle . . . Then suddenly, everything around her seemed to blur as she caught sight of Him for the first time "face-to-face."

He stood tall and gentle on the platform at the end of the aisle, patiently and lovingly waiting for His bride to approach. There were no bridesmaids or groomsmen; only her Prince Jesus and what appeared to be stacks and stacks of wedding presents. She had heard that He had prepared many gifts for His bride, but this was truly overwhelming. She always knew her emotions would run wild on her wedding day, but nothing had prepared her for the intense flood that filled and overflowed her heart at that moment.

As she approached her Groom—her Prince—she felt her heart race and her face become flush with shame and embarrassment. It hit her suddenly like a stabbing jolt of reality: He had done everything to prepare for this day. *He did everything to woo me, to bless me, to capture my heart, and now He is here to rescue me . . . and I have done nothing for Him during my life!*

She felt she had nothing to offer Him. No gifts. No guests. She reflected back on her life and realized she had labored and sweated over all the wrong things and for all the wrong reasons. She grabbed the hem of her gown ready to run away.

It was then that her eyes met His. There in His eyes she saw something in His gaze that was more intense than her shame, more powerful than her guilt. That "something" was greater than anything she had ever felt before. She turned back toward Him and slowly continued down the aisle.

Then it happened. Not all at once, but gradually. As she walked . . . as she approached her Prince . . . as she stared into His loving eyes . . . her shame began to melt away. Now she could see it: the look on His face was one of pure love, the kind of love that says, "You are mine, and nothing you have said or done can keep us apart . . . My Princess."

As the bride-to-be stepped up to stand next to her Groom, her Lord, every negative emotion loosed its grip on her and departed forever. Every pain that had burrowed its way into her soul disappeared once and for all. As she stood there in His presence, face-to-face, He smiled tenderly and gently wiped away the tears from her cheek, embraced His new bride, and said . . .

"You will never cry again, My love . . . Welcome home!"

His Princess Prayer

Dear Jesus,

What a strange and wondrous thought to think of You, my God, as my eternal husband. There is something so astonishing about discovering I am Your bride, the Bride of Christ. Please, Lord, lift the veil from my eyes and let me see You as my Prince. I want to let You into my heart. You are the true love my heart has longed for all my life. So today I stand at Your altar ready to surrender my heart, my soul, all that I am. May the rest of my days be lived preparing for Your return.

In Your name I pray, Amen!

His Princess in Action

Read the love letter below from *His Princess Bride* and bask in His love and truth.

My Beautiful Bride

You are so beautiful to Me. I wish for one moment that you could see what I see when I look at you. When I gaze at you, I see a treasure ready to be discovered, a princess ready to shine, and a bride ready to be loved. When I look at you . . . I love what I see! If you could grasp how beautiful you are in My eyes, then you would never feel insecure again. The beauty I created you to be is a reflection of Me, My love. I created you in My image, so never doubt again that your eternal beauty is a breath of heaven!

Love,
Your adoring Prince

For your royal husband delights in your beauty;
honor him, for he is your lord.

Psalm 45:11 NLT[2]

Treasure of Truth for Today

You have a real Prince preparing a place for you
to live happily ever after!

Day 29

Move On!

Forget the former things;
do not dwell on the past.
See, I am doing a new thing!
Isaiah 43:18–19

Move On from Insecurity

Queen Esther . . . had to move on from her identity as a power-less orphan and accept God's call to be queen. If she had focused on how unqualified she was to reign, she would have missed the opportunity to save the Jewish people and be a part of God's great eternal plan for His chosen ones.

Move On from Your Past Mistakes

King David . . . had to move on from his sins of adultery and murder. He cried out to God and received His forgiveness. God is so full of grace that He made something good out of David's bad choice by giving him and Bathsheba King Solomon once they repented and moved on.

MOVE ON FROM GUILT

The apostle Peter . . . had to move on when he failed to stand up for his Savior. Even though he loved Jesus passionately, Peter

His Princess Love Letter

My Princess,

Forget the former things! All have sinned and fallen short of My glory. If you've confessed your sins, I've forgiven them, so move on! I gave My life so you could be free from your past and live a new life in Me. Forgive those who have hurt you, and most important, forgive yourself. There is no wrong great enough to keep Me from redeeming you. Read My Word, My love. All My chosen ones have made mistakes and have gone through trials. I was with them, and I am with you today. I am ready to do a new thing in you, so trust Me to work out the things that have gone wrong in the past. It's time for you to move forward and do what I sent you here to do.

Love,
Your Savior, Jesus

denied Him not once, not twice, but three times. If Peter had not accepted God's forgiveness, then he might have spent his entire life paralyzed by guilt rather than helping other Jews realize that Jesus was their long-awaited Messiah. When we let guilt keep us paralyzed from living out our purpose, we are saying by our actions that the cross was not enough to set us free from the guilt of our past mistakes.

Move On from Pride

The apostle Paul could have allowed pride to keep him from his call. But God loved him so much that He allowed physical blindness to humble him. Many times God allows painful circumstances to break us of our pride and prepare us to become great, humble, holy women of God.

His Princess Prayer

My Lord,
   Thank You for Your life given for my mistakes.
Right now I receive Your gift of a new day and a new
life. It is amazing that all I have ever done wrong
is lost in Your sea of forgetfulness. May I never look
back again at who I was. Help me to move on and
move into Your plan for my life.
   In Your name I pray, Amen

His Princess in Action

Write down whatever guilt you are carrying right now and throw it in the trash. Do not let the devil whisper lies that you are still guilty—let your Lord whisper His truth that you are totally forgiven and a brand-new creation in Christ. Thank God now that you are new from the inside out!

Therefore, if anyone is in Christ, he is a new creation; the old has gone, the new has come!

2 Corinthians 5:17

Treasure of Truth for Today

Don't let your past torment you . . . let it teach you.
Leave the past where it belongs . . . at the cross.

Day 30

Leave a Legacy

For the LORD is good and his love endures forever;
his faithfulness continues through all generations.

Psalm 100:5

everal years ago, I had the privilege of knowing a true princess. Rachel was thirteen years old when she was diagnosed with cancer. She knew she was a daughter of the King, and she did not allow her illness to stop her from living out her royal call. She also knew God could heal her, but she loved her King so much that she said, "I will finish what God has called me to do, even if He doesn't heal me." I'll never forget what she said to me when I called to encourage her.

"Sheri, I don't know how much longer I have here on earth, so I need to hurry and tell as many of my classmates as possible about Jesus." She asked her family to pray for her every day, not just for healing, but for a divine appointment. Her pain gave her power.

Every day for three years, this little princess had a divine appointment at her high school. The kids could not understand why Rachel was so concerned about them when she was the one dying of cancer. On her sixteenth birthday, she announced, "I'm ready to go home to be with the Lord. I just want to see my high school class in heaven someday."

That night Rachel wrote a letter to her classmates. A few weeks later she went home to be with the Lord. Her final request, before she died, was that her classmates would attend her funeral. Rachel had been such a light in the darkness at her high school that the principal made buses available for the kids to attend her funeral. The pastor read Rachel's final letter to the huge gathering. It said,

> *Do not mourn for me, for today I am in God's kingdom, where there is no more sickness, no more pain, and no more death. My only prayer is that I will see you one day on the other side of eternity in Heaven, my Savior Jesus Christ made the way for you to get there.*

Then the pastor asked the kids, "How many of you want to go to heaven when you die?" Hundreds came forward and gave their lives to Jesus Christ. You see, one of God's princesses with cancer affected hundreds of lives. Just think how many of those young people were changed forever and became godly examples for their families and their communities.

Here's how I pray for you:

His Princess Prayer for You

Dear Lord,
Open my Sister Princess's eyes that she would see you in a way like never before. Take her tears and turn them into passion to do something to touch someone's life for You. Take all the pain that has

*burrowed its way into her soul, and pour Your love
over her and heal whatever is broken. Restore to her
whatever has been stolen from her by the enemy.
And may she finish strong and leave a legacy with
her life. Let all of the above come into Your full
purpose for her life.*

In Jesus' name, Amen

His Princess in Action

Write down in the front of your Bible what you want to be
remembered for when you're gone and date it. Then look at it
often.

Conclusion

His Princess in Action

Anyone can choose to be a worldly princess, but you, my Sister Princess, have been handpicked by the King to be His Princess. Now take your God-given appointed position. Let your life lived for your Lord be the legacy you leave behind!

My Closing Prayer for You

I pray that you will do your very best and allow God to do the rest. I pray that you will stay motivated to take care of God's temple, your body. I pray that you will remain real with God so that He can continue to heal your every hurt and share in your every joy. I pray that you will use your God-given gifts to be a present to those around you. I pray you will never lose sight of who you are in Christ, a daughter of the King, a special Princess created in His image. I pray you will experience the excitement of your adventures with the King by keeping your daily divine appointments. May He continue to strengthen you in your journey to excellence.

My final prayer for you is found in Psalm 20:4–5:

May he give you the desire of your heart
and make all your plans succeed.
We will shout for joy when you are victorious
and will lift up our banners in the name of our God.

I look forward to the day we can celebrate
together on the other side of eternity.

Now glory be to God! By his mighty power at work within us, he
is able to accomplish infinitely more than we would ever dare
to ask or hope.

Ephesians 3:20 NLT[1]

Treasure of Truth for Today

A worldly princess . . . glorifies herself.

His Princess . . . glorifies her King.

A worldly princess . . . cares about her needs and desires.

His Princess . . . is more concerned about the needs of others.

A worldly princess . . . will be known for staying in her own comfort zone.

His Princess . . . will be known for her character and courage.

A worldly princess . . . invests her time and talent for the praise of man.

His Princess . . . invests her time and talent for the praise of God.

A worldly princess's reign . . . will end soon.

His Princess's Reign . . . Will Last Forever!!!

His Princess
Meal Plan & Recipes

Preparation

Preparing to Fast

The following pages contain some amazing tasty and healthy recipes I have found to be of great joy to eat. You may use all these recipes throughout your 30-day fast, or you may use your own.

Remember, the Fast Is . . .

- Off all . . . corn, white potato, white rice

   But brown rice and brown rice pasta is fine
- Off all . . . white and brown sugar

   But Stevia, honey, molasses, pure maple syrup, and birch sugar (also known as xylitol) are fine
- Off all . . . bleached white flour

   But brown rice flour and/or spelt flour is fine, and yeast-free is best

- Off all . . . artificial sweeteners (no Splenda, no NutraSweet, no saccharin)
- Off all . . . diet artificial foods, **nothing** with MSG, saturated fats, fake fats, hydrogenated oils
- Off all . . . diet artificial drinks

    See Royally Refreshing Drinks for great refreshing healthy drinks

PREPARING FOR BATTLE

It's challenging to make time to prepare the proper foods and resist the fast-food drive-thrus—called "fast food" because it's better to fast than to eat the food! However, preparing in advance is essential. Try these preparation tips:

- Pick one day a week and do all your preparations at once.
- Cut up raw vegetables and put them in plastic bags. I wash my lettuce, dry it thoroughly with paper towels, and store it in plastic bags.
- Cut up fresh fruit and soak in lemon juice.
- Boil six to eight hormone-free eggs for quick protein snacks or to use in salads.
- Make two dozen healthy muffins (see muffin recipes) and put in freezer.
- Steam four to six cups of brown rice and store in plasticware in the refrigerator. I use brown rice for stir-fry with vegetables and chicken breast or plain with a meal.
- Boil four to six chicken breasts (hormone-free), then let them cool, dice them up, and store in plastic bags in the

refrigerator, or in the freezer for later use. These are used in salads and for stir-fry.

- Take two cups of nonfat plain yogurt, mix with any favorite seasoning, and use for veggie dip.
- Make a gallon of decaffeinated, fruit-flavored iced tea and add fruit juice and fresh lemons. Store in the refrigerator for a refreshing drink.
- Make sure that there is a big bowl of fresh fruit set out on a table.
- Place two quarts of distilled water in the refrigerator each morning, and make a goal to finish it off before going to bed.

Recipe Contents

BREAKFAST BUFFET
FOR HIS BEAUTY

Spinach, Tomato & Goat Cheese Omelet

1 tsp	extra-virgin olive oil
5	cherry tomatoes, halved
1	green onion, diced
1 cup	baby spinach, washed and patted dry
2	eggs
3	egg whites or ¼ cup egg substitute
¼ cup	crumbled goat cheese or low-fat jack shredded cheese
⅛ tsp	sea salt
⅛ tsp	freshly ground pepper
1 Tbl	water

Spray a small nonstick skillet with cooking spray. Add oil and heat over medium-high heat. Add tomatoes and green onion and cook, stirring once or twice, until softened, 1 to 2 minutes. Place spinach on top, cover, and let wilt, about 30 seconds. Stir to combine.

Whisk eggs with egg whites or egg substitute, reduce heat to medium-low and continue cooking, stirring constantly with a heatproof rubber spatula until the egg is starting to set, about 20 seconds. Continue cooking, lifting the edges so the uncooked egg will flow underneath, until mostly set, about 30 seconds more.

Sprinkle cheese, sea salt, and pepper over the omelet. Lift up an edge of the omelet and drizzle 1 tablespoon water under it. Cover, reduce heat to low, and cook until the egg is completely set and the cheese is melted, about 2 minutes. Fold over using the spatula and serve.

2 servings

French Toast Fit for a Princess

2	large eggs or 4 egg whites
1½ cups	vanilla almond milk or soy vanilla milk
1 packet	Stevia sweetener
½ tsp	cinnamon
¼ tsp	nutmeg
½ Tbl	vanilla extract
	grape seed oil, as needed
8 slices	gluten-free bread
	pure maple syrup (not corn syrup)

Whisk together the eggs, milk, Stevia, cinnamon, nutmeg, and vanilla until thoroughly mixed.

Heat a griddle or large frying pan generously greased with grape seed oil until hot but not smoking.

Soak the bread slices in the egg mixture until moistened. Place the soaked slices on the griddle. Discard any excess egg mixture.

When the bottoms are golden brown, flip with a spatula and brown the other side. Keep them in a warm oven until ready to serve.

Drizzle maple syrup and enjoy!

4 servings

Granny's Apple Muffins

6 Tbl	grape seed oil
1 tsp	butter flavoring or Butter Buds
1 cup	birch sugar or honey
2	eggs or 4 egg whites
1½ tsp	vanilla extract
1 cup	brown rice flour
1 cup	spelt flour
½ tsp	baking powder (non-aluminum)
½ tsp	baking soda (non-aluminum)
½ tsp	sea salt
⅓ cup	unsweetened applesauce
⅔ cup	nonfat, nondairy sour cream
2	Gala or Granny Smith apples, peeled, cored, and sliced

Preheat the oven to 350° and spray a muffin tin with nonstick spray.

In a large bowl, beat grape seed oil, butter flavoring, and birch sugar or honey together with an electric mixer on high speed until the mixture is light in color and fluffy.

Decrease the speed to low and add the eggs one at a time. Add the vanilla.

In a separate bowl, combine the flours, baking powder, baking soda, and salt.

Fold half of the dry ingredients into the butter mixture using a rubber spatula or wooden spoon. Stir in the applesauce and sour cream. Fold in the remaining dry ingredients.

Fill the muffin tins halfway with batter. Add a few apple slices to each muffin and spoon the remaining batter over the apples.

Bake on the center rack until the muffins are golden brown and springy to the touch, about 35 to 40 minutes.

Yields approx. 1 dozen muffins

Fresh Tomato & Asparagus Frittata

Serve this beautiful egg dish right from the skillet.

½ pound	fresh asparagus spears, trimmed
¼ cup	butter
1 cup	fresh mushrooms, sliced
1 medium	onion, chopped (½ cup)
6	eggs or 10 egg whites
8 slices	turkey bacon, cooked, crumbled (⅔ cup)
1 small	tomato, sliced
4 ounces	shredded low-fat or goat cheddar cheese (1 cup)

Place asparagus spears in nonstick 10-inch skillet; add enough water to cover. Bring to a full boil. Cook over medium heat until crisply tender, 5 to 7 minutes. Drain; transfer asparagus to small plate.

Melt butter in same skillet until sizzling. Add mushrooms and onion; cook over medium heat until tender, 3 to 4 minutes.

Beat eggs in medium bowl until frothy; stir in bacon. Pour into skillet. Stir gently over medium heat to cook evenly on bottom, 3 to 4 minutes. As egg mixture sets, lift edges with spatula to allow uncooked egg to flow underneath. Arrange tomato slices and asparagus on top. Cover; continue cooking until eggs are set, 4 to 5 minutes. Sprinkle with cheese; cut into wedges (like a pizza slice).

What you don't eat put in baggies to eat throughout the week.

6 servings

Recipe Tip

Any combination of cooked broccoli, green bell pepper, red bell pepper, carrot, zucchini, or summer squash can be substituted for tomato or asparagus.

Roasted Red Pepper Frittata

2 slices	turkey bacon, cut into 1-inch pieces
½ cup	yellow onion, chopped
2 cups	mushrooms, sliced
½ cup	roasted red pepper in a jar
2 small	zucchini squash, sliced ¼-inch thick
1 tsp	basil
	sea salt to taste
	pepper to taste
2	eggs
½ cup	shredded cheddar goat cheese or low-fat Swiss cheese

In a large skillet, cook the bacon over medium heat until it is lightly browned. Remove the bacon with a slotted spoon and reserve. Drain all but 1 teaspoon of the bacon fat from the skillet.

Add the onion to the skillet and cook for 2 minutes. Add the mushrooms and peppers and cook for 2 more minutes. Add the zucchini and basil and cook until the vegetables are soft, about 3 more minutes. Season well with salt and pepper.

Pour the eggs into the skillet and cover. Cook (without stirring) for 5 minutes.

Remove the cover and sprinkle the cheese and reserved bacon over the top of the frittata. Cover and cook until the cheese is melted, about 2 minutes. Remove from heat and slice into 6 wedges. Serve immediately.

2 servings

Berry Nut Muffins

2 cups	brown rice flour (Pamela's Baking & Pancake Mix is best)
1 cup	birch sugar or honey
2 tsp	baking powder
¼ tsp	sea salt
2 large	eggs, room temperature
1 cup	unsweetened soy or almond milk, room temperature
4 Tbl	grape seed oil
½ cup	chopped, dried cranberries or dried blueberries
½ cup	finely chopped pecans or walnuts

Preheat oven to 400°. Coat a muffin pan with nonstick spray.

Sift the flour, sugar, baking powder, and salt together in large bowl. (This can be done the night before and kept covered on the counter.)

Whisk together the eggs, milk, and oil. If the eggs and milk are cold, the oil may solidify.

Make a well in the center of the dry ingredients and add the liquid all at once. Stir with a wooden spoon until the dry ingredients are just moistened. Fold in the berries and nuts. The batter will be a little lumpy; do not overmix.

Fill the tins two-thirds full, being careful not to drip batter on the edge of the tins where it will burn and cause sticking.

Bake until golden brown and set in the center, approximately 12 to 15 minutes. The muffins are done when a small knife inserted in the center of a muffin comes out dry. Cool for 5 minutes before removing from the pan.

Yields 1 dozen muffins

Fantastic Tomato Zucchini Frittata

¼ cup	canned coconut milk
1 medium	onion, chopped
6	fresh eggs, slightly beaten
½ tsp	dried basil leaves
¼ tsp	sea salt
¼ tsp	coarsely ground pepper
3 Tbl	butter
½ tsp	finely chopped fresh garlic
1 medium	zucchini, diagonally sliced ¼-inch thick
1 medium	tomato, cut into 6 slices
2 ounces	low-fat shredded mozzarella cheese (½ cup)
2 Tbl	freshly grated Parmesan cheese

Heat oven to 350°. Combine milk, onion, eggs, basil, sea salt, and pepper in medium bowl.

Melt butter in 10-inch ovenproof skillet until sizzling; add garlic. Cook over medium heat until garlic is tender, 2 to 3 minutes. Pour egg mixture into skillet.

Bake for 8 to 10 minutes or until egg mixture is partially set. Remove from oven.

Arrange zucchini slices in circle on top of egg mixture; place tomato slices on top of zucchini. Sprinkle with mozzarella and Parmesan cheese. Continue baking for 10 to 14 minutes or until cheese is melted and eggs are set.

6 servings

Lovely Lunches
for His Princess

Steak & Kiwi Salad

5 ounces	lean steak
1 head	bib lettuce
1 can (8 ounces)	water chestnuts, sliced and drained
2	grapefruit, peeled and sectioned
1	avocado
4	kiwis, peeled and sliced
1 cup	cucumbers, sliced

SHERRY VINAIGRETTE DRESSING

3 Tbl	sherry vinegar
1 Tbl	Dijon mustard
2 Tbl	extra virgin olive oil
1 Tbl	honey
	pinch of sea salt
	freshly ground black pepper

Spray steak with cooking spray and add a dash of sea salt. Broil, let cool for 10 minutes, then thinly slice.

Gently wash and dry the bib lettuce and water chestnuts.

Peel the grapefruit and remove the sections.

Peel the avocado and slice into sections.

Peel the kiwi and slice into sections

Place the ingredients for the vinaigrette in a bowl and whisk to combine. Gently toss the bib lettuce with the vinaigrette.

Make a bed of bib lettuce and sliced cucumbers on each plate. Arrange the grapefruit and avocado sections on top. Place the kiwi slices in the center. Then add steak to top it off, and drizzle with leftover vinaigrette.

Serving size: about 1 cup of salad with 1 tablespoon vinaigrette

Chicken Salad Delight

½ cup	birch sugar or honey
½ cup	fresh lemon juice
2 tsp	yellow onion, diced
1 tsp	Dijon-style prepared mustard
½ tsp	sea salt
⅔ cup	grape seed oil
1 Tbl	poppy seeds
1 head	romaine lettuce, torn into bite-size pieces
4 ounces	crumbled goat cheese or shredded low-fat Swiss cheese (1 cup)
1 cup	raw unsalted cashews
¼ cup	dried unsweetened cranberries
1	green apple, peeled, cored, and diced
1	pear, peeled, cored, and sliced
1	cooked chicken breast, diced

In a blender or food processor, combine birch sugar or honey, lemon juice, onion, mustard, and sea salt. Process until well blended. With machine still running, add oil in a slow, steady stream until mixture is thick and smooth. Add poppy seeds, and process just a few seconds more to mix.

In a large serving bowl, toss together the romaine lettuce, crumbled goat cheese, cashews, dried cranberries, apple, pear, and chicken. Pour dressing over salad just before serving, and toss to coat.

4 to 6 servings

Delicious Orange & Green Supreme

7 cups	field greens lettuce
2 cups	celery (about 4 pieces), chopped
1 cup	fresh orange sections, sliced
1 cup	radishes, thinly sliced
¼ cup	green onions, thinly sliced
2 Tbl	white wine vinegar
2 Tbl	fresh orange juice
1 Tbl	light-colored sesame oil
¼ tsp	sea salt
⅛ tsp	black pepper

Combine first 5 ingredients in a large bowl. Combine vinegar, juice, oil, sea salt, and pepper in a small bowl; stir with a whisk. Pour over salad, tossing gently to coat. Serve immediately.

5 to 6 servings (serving size: 2 cups)

Salad Greens of Grace

1 cup	cooked chicken breast, diced
4 cups	of raw spinach leaves
1 cup	red cabbage, thinly sliced
¼ cup	green onion, diced
1	cucumber, seeded and sliced
½ cup	chopped walnuts or pecans
¼ cup	Gorgonzola cheese, crumbled
1	tart green apple, cored and diced

VINAIGRETTE DRESSING

3 Tbl	sherry or balsamic vinegar
1 Tbl	Dijon mustard
2 Tbl	extra-virgin olive oil
1 Tbl	honey
1 pinch	sea salt
1 pinch	freshly ground black pepper

In a large bowl, combine all salad ingredients.

Combine all dressing ingredients in a dressing bottle and shake.

Pour desired amount of dressing over salad; toss and serve.

2 servings

Awesome Chicken, Apricot & Cabbage Salad

3 cups	cooked chicken breast, diced
1 head	purple cabbage, sliced very thinly
½ head	green cabbage, sliced very thinly
4	fresh apricots, seeded, coarsely chopped
⅓ cup	green onions, chopped

DRESSING

⅓ cup	nonfat sour cream or nondairy sour cream
¼ cup	nonfat plain yogurt
¼ cup	fresh-squeezed orange juice
1 packet	Stevia sweetener
½ tsp	sea salt
¼ tsp	nutmeg

Combine all dressing ingredients in small bowl. Whisk together briskly. Set aside.

Combine all salad ingredients in large bowl. Add dressing to salad; toss to coat.

6 to 8 servings (store uneaten portion in Tupperware for the next few days)

Victory Veggie Slaw

The colorful mix of vegetables in this coleslaw recipe is a new twist on an old favorite.

2 medium	carrots, shredded (1 cup)
1 medium	green onion, finely diced (½ cup)
1 small head	green cabbage, shredded (2 cups)
1 small	jicama, shredded (1½ cups)
1 small head	red cabbage, shredded (2 cups)

DRESSING

½ cup	nondairy sour cream
½ cup	lowfat mayonnaise
2 tsp	celery seed
1 Tbl	prepared horseradish
¼ tsp	sea salt
¼ tsp	coarsely ground pepper

Combine all dressing ingredients in small bowl. Cover; refrigerate at least 30 minutes.

Meanwhile, combine carrots, onions, green cabbage, and jicama in medium bowl. Drain, pressing out excess moisture.

Add red cabbage to vegetable mixture. Pour dressing over salad; toss to coat well. Serve immediately. Store refrigerated.

8 servings

"Extreme Health in a Bottle" Dressing

    1 cup   apple cider vinegar
    1 cup   Braggs Liquid Aminos amino acid
    ¼ cup honey

Combine ingredients and shake well.

RECIPES FOR DINING
WITH THE KING

Royal Warm Chicken Salad

6 cups	gourmet salad greens
½ cup	red cabbage, thinly sliced
1	warm cooked or broiled chicken breast, diced
¼ tsp	allspice
	salt & pepper to taste
3 Tbl	unsweetened dried cranberries
1 Tbl	toasted pecans and/or hazelnuts, coarsely chopped

VINAIGRETTE DRESSING

2 Tbl	raspberry-flavored vinegar
3 Tbl	water
1½ tsp	grape seed oil
¼ tsp	sea salt
⅛ tsp	pepper

Combine salad greens and cabbage in a bowl.

In a separate bowl, combine vinaigrette dressing ingredients and stir well with a whisk. Reserve 1 tablespoon vinaigrette; set aside. Pour remaining vinaigrette over greens mixture, tossing gently to coat.

Season chicken with allspice, salt, and pepper.

Then sprinkle cranberries, diced chicken, and nuts over greens. Drizzle reserved vinaigrette over salad.

4 servings

179

Sizzling Steak Salad

                1 (16-ounce) flank steak, trimmed
                       ½ tsp sea salt
                       ¼ tsp freshly ground black pepper
                       2 Tbl white wine vinegar
                       1 Tbl water
                       2 tsp extra-virgin olive oil
                       ¼ tsp sea salt
                       ¼ tsp freshly ground black pepper
                       ⅛ tsp birch sugar or honey
                     6 cups spinach leaves
                 4 medium tomatoes, each cut into 6 wedges
                         2 hard-cooked large eggs, each cut into 4
                            wedges

Sprinkle both sides of steak with ½ teaspoon sea salt and ¼ teaspoon pepper. Prepare grill or broiler.

Place steak on BBQ grill rack or under broiler that is coated with cooking spray; grill 4–5 minutes on each side or until desired degree of doneness. Remove steak from grill or broiler. Lightly cover steak with foil; let stand 10 minutes. Cut steak diagonally across the grain into thin slices.

Combine vinegar and next 5 ingredients in a medium bowl; stir with a whisk. Add spinach; toss well. Serve with 3–6 ounces of steak, 6 tomato wedges, and 2 egg wedges.

4 to 6 servings

Kingdom Kabobs

DRY RUB

1 tsp	cinnamon
½ tsp	sea salt
½ tsp	cumin
½ tsp	turmeric
¼ tsp	cayenne (optional)
¼ tsp	pepper
¼ tsp	cardamom
⅛ tsp	ground cloves
⅛ tsp	nutmeg
2 tsp	raw sugar

KABOBS

2 pounds	boneless, skinless chicken breasts
2 small	red onions, peeled and cut into 1-inch-wide sections
2	bell peppers, cleaned and cut into 1-inch squares
¼ cup	olive oil
	sea salt
	pepper
12	bamboo skewers (10-inch), soaked in water for 30 minutes

In a small bowl, combine the dry rub ingredients and mix well.

Cut the meat into 1½-inch cubes and put them in a gallon-size ziplock bag with the rub mix. Seal the bag and shake it vigorously until all the chicken is well coated.

Place the onions and peppers in a gallon-size zip-lock bag, add the olive oil, and season with salt and pepper. Seal the bag and shake it vigorously to coat the vegetables well.

Assemble the kabobs by alternately skewering pieces of chicken, onions, and peppers.

Prepare a charcoal fire or set a gas grill to medium-high, close the lid, and heat until hot.

Grill the kabobs, turning occasionally, until the chicken is no longer pink inside, about 8 to 10 minutes on a gas grill.

6 to 8 servings

Crowning Cauliflower Chicken Soup

1 Tbl	olive oil
1 cup	finely chopped celery
1 large	onion, chopped
½ tsp	curry powder
½ tsp	fresh garlic, diced
2 tsp	sea salt
1 tsp	freshly ground black pepper
1 small	russet potato
about 1½ quarts	low-sodium chicken broth or vegetable broth
6 cups	cauliflower florets
¼ cup	chopped fresh parsley
4 Tbl	nondairy sour cream
2 cups	cooked chicken breast, diced

Heat the olive oil in a saucepan over medium-low heat. Add the celery, onion, curry powder, and garlic; season lightly with sea salt and pepper; and cook for 10 minutes.

Peel and slice the potato and add it to the pot. Add broth and bring to a boil quickly over high heat.

Lower the heat and simmer until the vegetables are completely tender, about 15 minutes.

Add the cauliflower and simmer until just tender, about 5 to 7 minutes.

Blend the parsley and sour cream together and set aside.

Remove soup from stove. Puree/blend lightly the soup in a blender until smooth and creamy, then add diced chicken breast and sea salt and pepper to taste.

Serve the soup in bowls with a dollop of parsley cream.

Serving size: about 1½ cups

Beauty of Broccoli with Grilled Wild Salmon

BROCCOLI RECIPE

½ stick	butter (¼ cup)
2 Tbl	coarsely chopped shallots or onion
2 tsp	chopped garlic
1 Tbl	balsamic vinegar
3 tsp	olive oil
7 cups	raw broccoli florets (organic, if possible)
1 medium	red bell pepper, cut into 1-inch pieces (1 cup)
1 tsp	sea salt
¼ tsp	pepper
3 Tbl	water
2 Tbl	crushed raw or toasted almonds

BROILED SALMON

4	fresh wild salmon fillets
	grape seed oil
	garlic powder
1	fresh lime

Melt butter in 2-quart heavy saucepan over medium heat. Cook, stirring constantly and watching closely, until butter turns golden brown (4 to 6 minutes). Remove from heat; stir in shallots, garlic, and vinegar. Set aside.

Place all remaining ingredients except water and crushed almonds in deep, 12-inch skillet. Cook over medium-high heat, stirring occasionally, 3 minutes. Add water; reduce heat to medium. Cover; continue cooking until broccoli is crisply tender (4 to 5 minutes). Remove from heat.

Stir browned butter mixture into broccoli. Sprinkle with crushed almonds if desired.

RECIPE TIP

To toast crushed almonds, place in shallow baking pan. Bake at 350°. for 6 to 8 minutes or until lightly browned.

BROILED SALMON FILLETS

Baste salmon with grape seed oil and sprinkle with garlic powder, then broil about 10 minutes per inch of thickness. When done, remove and squeeze fresh lime over it.

Serve with broccoli dish.

4 servings

Glazed Asparagus & Yams with Halibut

ASPARAGUS RECIPE

1 cup	water
1 pound	fresh asparagus spears, trimmed
3 large	yams, sliced diagonally ¼ inch thick (2 cups)
¼ cup	butter
3 Tbl	water
1 Tbl	fresh-squeezed lemon juice
1 tsp	cornstarch
1 tsp	freshly grated lemon peel
2 Tbl	chopped pecans, toasted or raw

BROILED HALIBUT

4	halibut fillets
	extra-virgin olive oil
	garlic powder
	fresh lemon wedges

Place 1 cup water in 10-inch skillet. Bring to a full boil, then reduce to medium heat; add asparagus and yams. Cover; continue cooking, stirring occasionally, until asparagus and yams are crisply tender, 7 to 9 minutes. Drain. Remove from skillet; keep warm.

Melt butter in same skillet. Stir together 3 tablespoons water, lemon juice, and cornstarch in small bowl; stir into butter. Cook over medium heat, stirring constantly, until sauce thickens, 2 to 3 minutes. Stir in lemon peel.

To serve, spoon sauce over warm asparagus and yams. Sprinkle with pecans.

186

BROILED HALIBUT

Baste halibut with olive oil and sprinkle with garlic powder, then broil 5–7 minutes or until it flakes easily with fork. Squeeze fresh lemons over it when served with asparagus and yams.

4 to 6 servings

SOUL-SOOTHING SNACKS

Happy Hawaiian Fruity Salad

1 packet	Stevia sweetener
1 Tbl	fresh-squeezed lemon juice
¼ tsp	vanilla
½ cup	raw almonds, diced
1 cup	nonfat plain yogurt
1 cup	fresh pineapple chunks
1 cup	celery, thinly sliced
1 medium	banana, sliced (⅔ cup)
1 medium	papaya, peeled, pitted, and cubed (1 cup)
	light sprinkles of toasted coconut, if desired

Blend Stevia, lemon juice, and vanilla in small cup. Gently toss together juice mixture and remaining ingredients, except toasted coconut, in large bowl. Sprinkle with toasted coconut. Serve immediately.

2 servings

Fruit Delight

1	red apple, cored and chopped
1	Granny Smith apple, cored and chopped
1	peach or nectarine, pitted and sliced
2 stalks	celery, chopped
½ cup	dried apricots, diced
¼ cup	dried cranberries
½ cup	chopped raw pecans or walnuts
1 (8-ounce)	plain or vanilla goats milk yogurt
½ packet	Stevia sweetener

In a large bowl, combine red apple, Granny Smith apple, peach or nectarine, celery, apricots, dried cranberries, and nuts. Stir Stevia into yogurt, then add yogurt to fruit and mix. Chill until ready to serve.

4–6 servings

Cheesy Snack Ball

8 ounces	tofu cream cheese, softened
8 ounces	reduced-fat cream cheese, softened
1	green onion, chopped
6 ounces	sliced smoked turkey, finely chopped
1 cup	slivered almonds

Mix cream cheeses together in a bowl. Add green onion and turkey to cream cheese. Cover and chill 1–2 hours. Shape into a ball and roll in slivered almonds.

Serve with brown rice or whole grain gluten-free crackers.

ROYALLY REFRESHING DRINKS

Minty Lime Cooler

½ cup   freshly squeezed lime juice
⅓ cup   birch sugar or honey or 1 packet Stevia
           sweetener
½ cup   packed mint leaves
1 (12-ounce) bottle sparkling water
      3   lime slices, for garnish
           mint leaves, for garnish

Combine the lime juice, sugar, and mint in a blender. Puree until smooth.

Fill 2 tall glasses half full with ice cubes. Pour half of the lime juice concentrate in each. Top with sparkling water, garnish with lime and mint, and serve.

Cranberry Spritzer

½ cup   chilled pure, naturally sweetened cranberry
juice
1 cup   chilled sparkling water
1   lime, cut into 4 wedges

Stir the cranberry juice and the water together in a small pitcher. Pour into large glasses filled with ice. Just before serving, add the lime wedges.

Tangy Tomato Refresher

1 cup   low-sodium V-8 juice
¼ cup   fresh carrot juice
1 Tbl   organic apple cider vinegar
1   fresh lemon
½ tsp   sea salt

Pour first 3 ingredients in a large glass, then squeeze in the entire lemon and stir in salt.

Royal Raspberry Tea

6 bags	raspberry-flavored black tea or raspberry herbal tea
¼ cup	fresh mint leaves
4 cups	cold water
2 droppers full	liquid Stevia sweetener
12	raspberries, for garnish
4	mint leaves, for garnish

Boil water in medium pot; add tea bags and mint and simmer for 3 minutes.

Strain the tea into a pitcher, add Stevia and stir; cover, and refrigerate until ready to serve.

When ready to serve, fill 4 tall glasses with ice. Fill the glasses with tea and garnish each glass with a few raspberries and a mint leaf.

Yields 1 quart

Princess Pineapple-Papaya Smoothie

1 scoop	egg white vanilla protein powder
½ cup	orange juice
¼ cup	pineapple, peeled, cored, and cubed
¼ cup	ripe papaya, peeled, seeded, and chopped
1 cup	ice

Place the juice, fruit, and protein powder in a blender.
Blend on high speed for 30 seconds.
Add the ice and blend until smooth.

Blueberry Protein Smoothie

¼ cup	vanilla almond milk
½ cup	plain, low-fat yogurt
½ cup	washed, stemmed blueberries
1 Tbl	honey
1 scoop	whey or egg white vanilla protein powder
1 cup	ice

Place all the ingredients in a blender. Blend on high speed
until smooth.

Royal Resource Guide

Solar Ray
Birch Sugar 1-800-the-meal
Jay Robb egg white protein
Braggs Apple Cider Vinegar
Braggs Liquid Aminos amino acids
Pamela's Gluten-free Mixes

For more resources and recipes please visit my
website at www.hisprincess.com.

Metric Conversion Guide

VOLUME

U.S. Units	Metric
½ teaspoon	2 ml
1 teaspoon	5 ml
1 tablespoon	20 ml
¼ cup	60 ml
⅓ cup	80 ml
½ cup	125 ml
⅔ cup	170 ml
¾ cup	190 ml
1 cup	250 ml
1 quart	1 liter

LENGTH

Inches	Centimeters
1	2.5
2	5.0
3	7.5
4	10.0
5	12.5
6	15.0
7	17.5
8	20.5
9	23.0
10	25.5
11	28.0
12	30.5
13	33.0
14	35.5
15	38.0

TEMPERATURE

Fahrenheit	Celsius
250°	120°
275°	140°
300°	150°
325°	160°
350°	180°
375°	190°
400°	200°
425°	220°
450°	230°
475°	240°
500°	260°

WEIGHT

U.S. Units	Metric
1 ounce	30 grams
2 ounces	60 grams
3 ounces	90 grams
4 ounces (¼ pound)	125 grams
8 ounces (½ pound)	225 grams
16 ounces (1 pound)	500 grams

Note: The recipes in this cookbook have not been developed or tested using metric measures. When converting recipes to metric, some variations in quality may be noted.

Sheri Rose Shepherd is the bestselling author of *His Princess: Love Letters from Your King*; *His Princess Bride: Love Letters from Your Prince*; and several other books. She has overcome a food addiction and an eating disorder and has lost over sixty pounds and kept if off for twenty years. Sheri Rose speaks to tens of thousands of women every year. Her story has been one of the most popular shows on *Focus on the Family*. Her weight story has also been featured on the *Billy Graham Primetime Television Special*, seen nationwide.

Visit www.fitformyking.com
or call (949) 609-3023 to find
additional resources, includin

- ❧ Dates and locations for Fit for My King Conferences
- ❧ Where to find a small group doing this study
- ❧ Resources to start your own small group
- ❧ Information about a companion DVD curriculum
- ❧ Inspiration from Sheri Rose Shepherd
- ❧ And more . . .

YOU'VE HEARD FROM YOUR KING.
Now it's time to hear from your Prince.

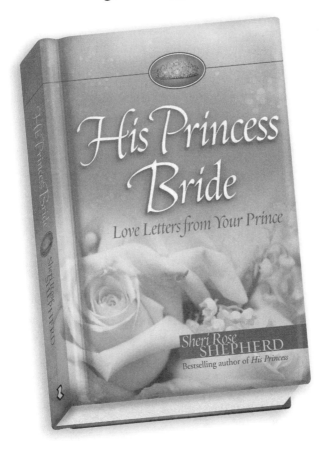

"Perfect for a gift, *His Princess Bride* will touch women's hearts at any age."
—*Christian Retailing*

His Princess SERIES

Strength and Power for Men from
JACOB A. SHEPHERD

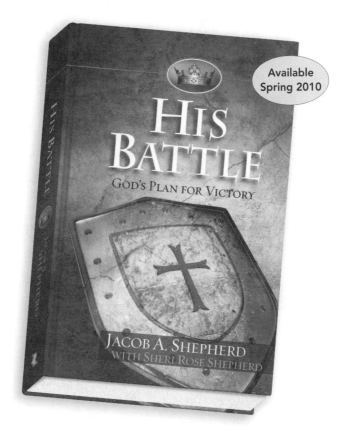

Available Spring 2010

HIS BATTLE

GOD'S PLAN FOR VICTORY

JACOB A. SHEPHERD
WITH SHERI ROSE SHEPHERD

Restore your God-given fight! Learn to walk and live
with power and truth again.